AF408377

# Wisconsin Through the Seasons

## Mid-Twentieth Century Landscapes

## as Seen by an Artist and Two of His Sons

*Text by Michael Grudzielanek*

ISBN: 979-8-218-39531-5

Library of Congress Control Number: 2024906019



Printed by IngramSpark in the United States of America

First printing, 2024

Prosna Banks Publishing, Milwaukee, Wisconsin

# CONTENTS

# ACKNOWLEDGMENTS

*A special thanks to each family member who contributed toward the making of this book. Your insight on the content was invaluable, and your care and preservation of the art has ensured that many more can now appreciate our relatives' works.*

Bradley and Arlene Angell
Gerald Angelski
Clare Ann Gaouette
Marlene Grudzielanek
Kristin and Graham Hildebrandt
Dorothy and Gerald Turow

# <u>INTRODUCTION</u>

Anyone who grew up in Wisconsin—or calls it home—remembers a cherished scene from his or her favorite season. It could be the silent beauty of the woods on a winter morning after snowfall, the earliest blooms of spring budding in the countryside, the sailboat-studded view of the Lake Michigan shore on a summer day, or the vibrant display of orange leaves against the autumn sky. Generations of Wisconsin artists have captured their fondest scenes on paper or canvas. Each time, they have preserved a snapshot from the crossroads of a unique place and time, one that has never quite looked the same since.

The period from the mid-1930's through the 1950's was nostalgic for those who remembered some of the original buildings that made Milwaukee's skyline before giving way to urban renewal. Timeworn farmhouses and weather-beaten barns stood stately in that era before they were removed—the fields and marshes of those decades replaced by today's subdivisions and shopping centers. Each passing season brought change to both the natural and man-made features of the landscape.

Milwaukee artist Thomas Angelski (1884-1973) began oil painting as an adult and refined his skills at the Layton School of Art. His oldest son Edward Angell (1910-2007) and a younger son Eugene Angelski (1919-2017) pursued their own lifelong interests in art, each with his own unique style. This book presents a selection of Angelski family artwork from the mid-1930's through the 1950's, including local scenes that were not only familiar to them but an integral part of their lives—from the farms of Marinette County (north of Green Bay) to the streets of Milwaukee and beyond.

When artists paint or sketch, they do more than merely capture an image; they try to capture a certain feeling associated with it so the observer can experience it too. The Angelski artists visually convey the same ambience as their Twentieth Century contemporary poets when we read their seasonal verses. As you enjoy these scenes through the eyes of the artists, they will move you to reflect on your own favorite times of the year and memories of special places you may recognize from many decades ago.

Michael Grudzielanek
Great-grandson of Thomas Angelski

# Wisconsin Through the Seasons

❖ *One must have a mind of winter*
*To regard the frost and the boughs*
*Of the pine-trees crusted with snow;*

*And have been cold a long time*
*To behold the junipers shagged with ice,*
*The spruces rough in the distant glitter*

*Of the January sun; and not to think*
*Of any misery in the sound of the wind,*
*In the sound of a few leaves,*

*Which is the sound of the land*
*Full of the same wind*
*That is blowing in the same bare place*

*For the listener, who listens in the snow,*
*And, nothing himself, beholds*
*Nothing that is not there and the nothing that is.*

—Wallace Stevens
"The Snow Man"

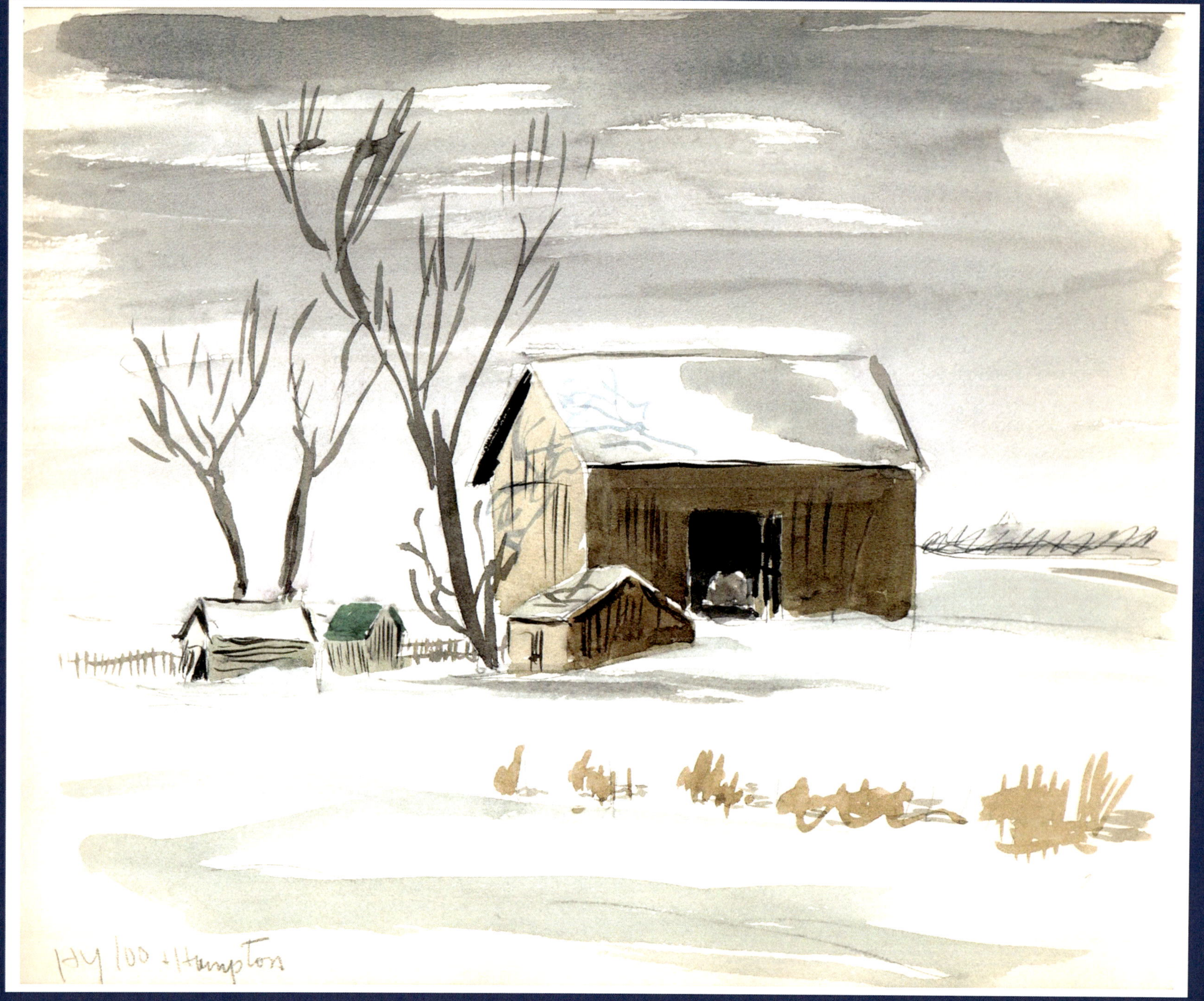


The day after snowfall in the country, one can scarcely tell where the field ends and the sky begins.

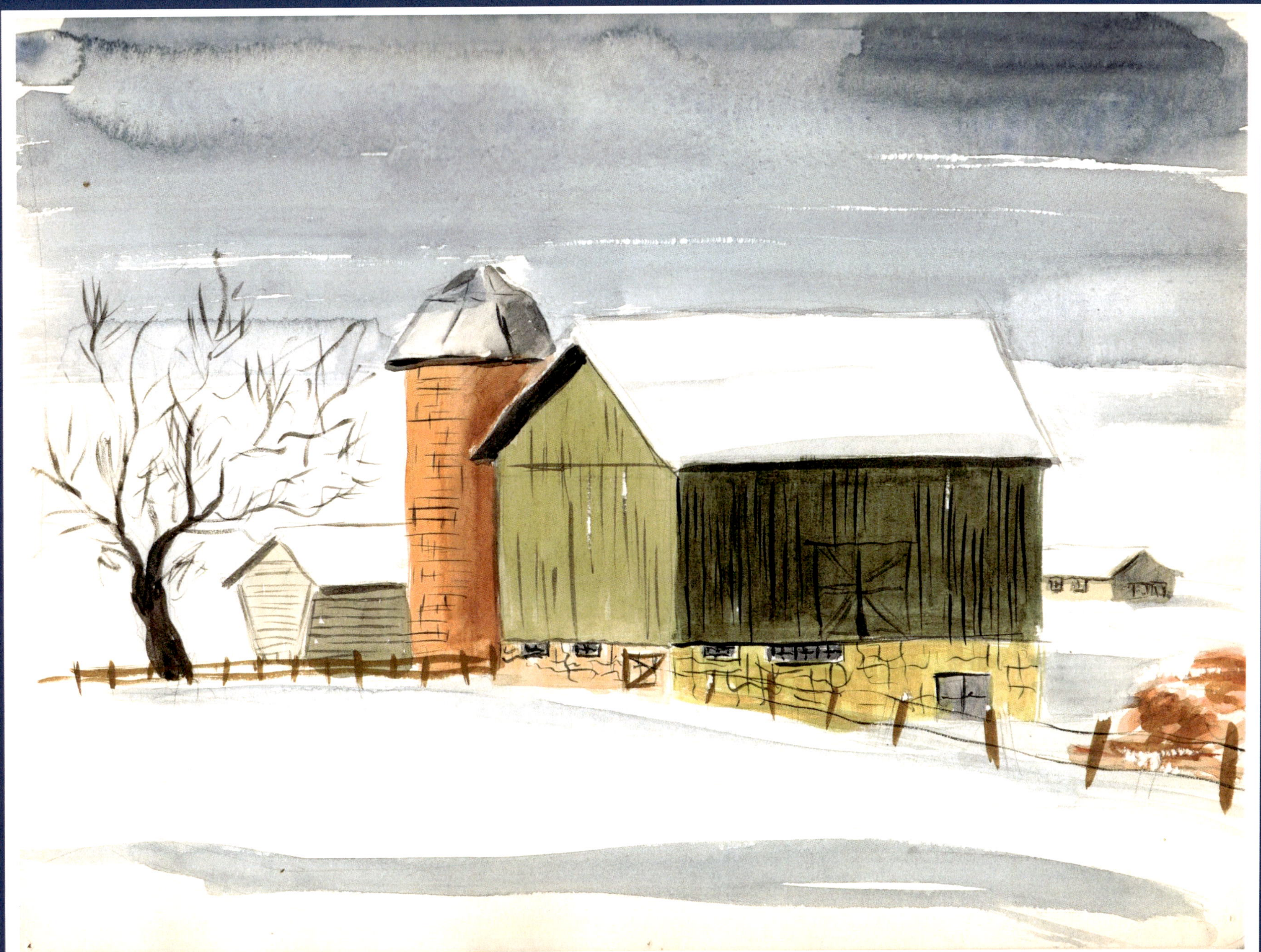

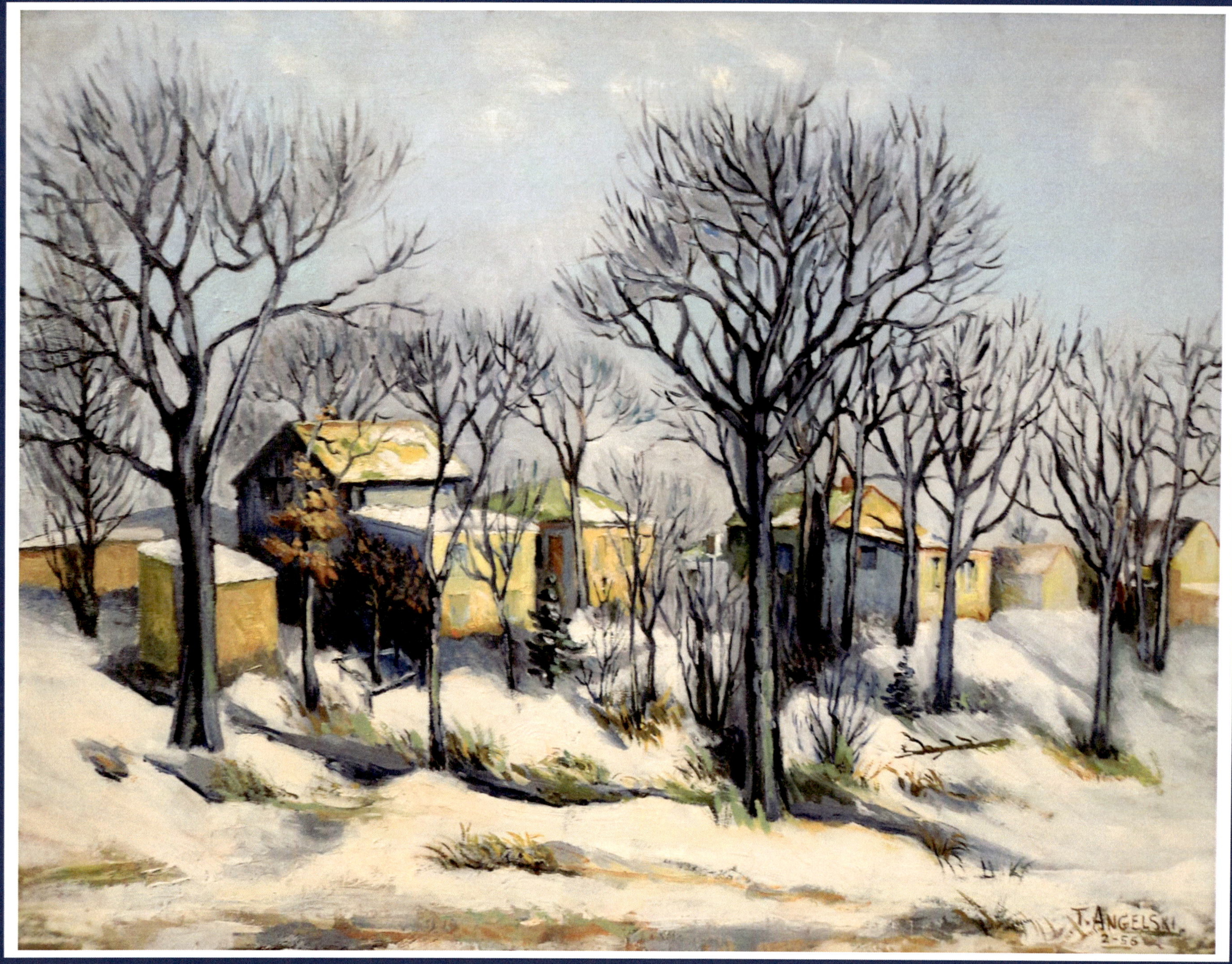

Snow clings to the eaves of suburban homes and the bare branches of trees both young and old.

As a boat plies the river in the
heart of the city, its steam
trails through the chilly air.

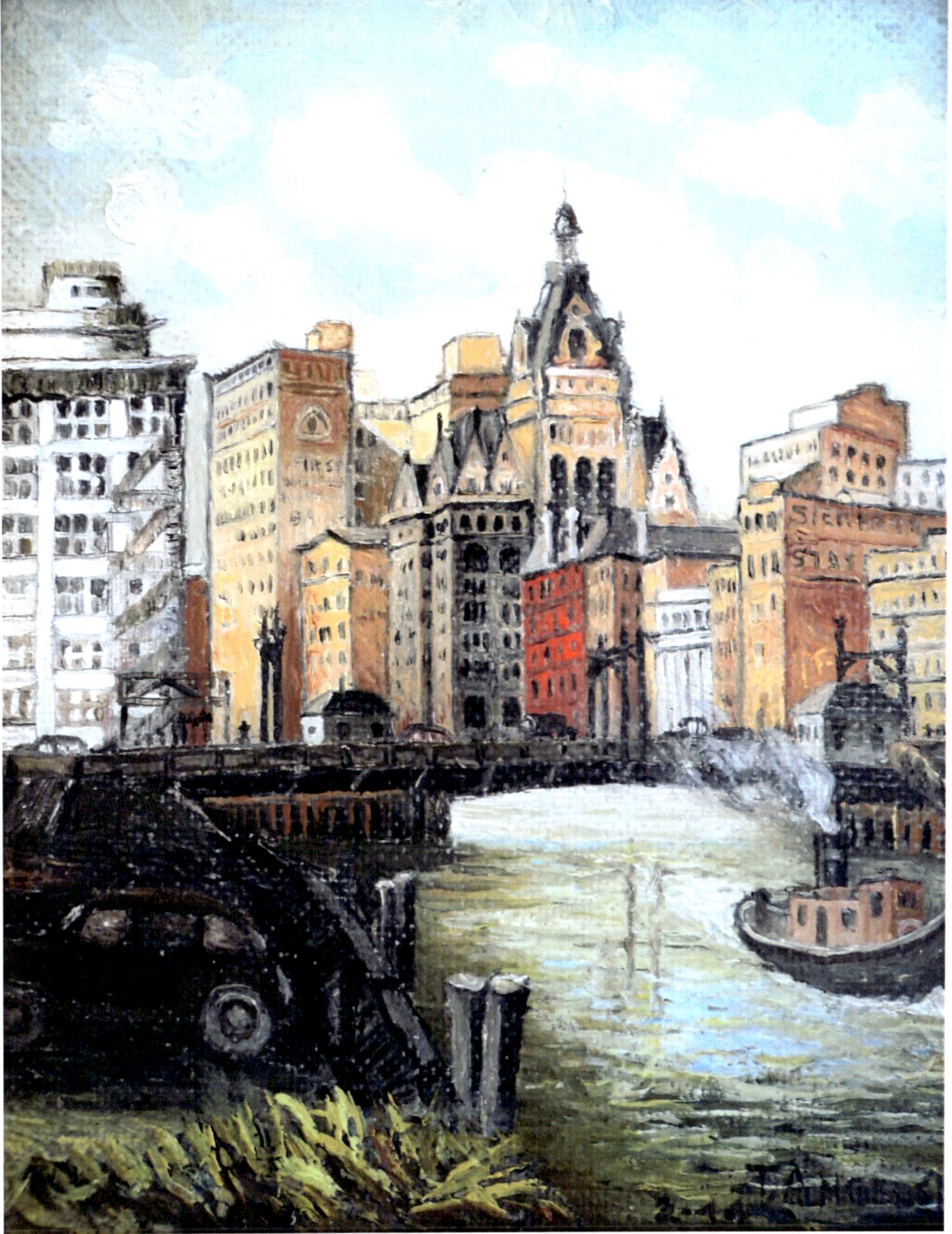

4

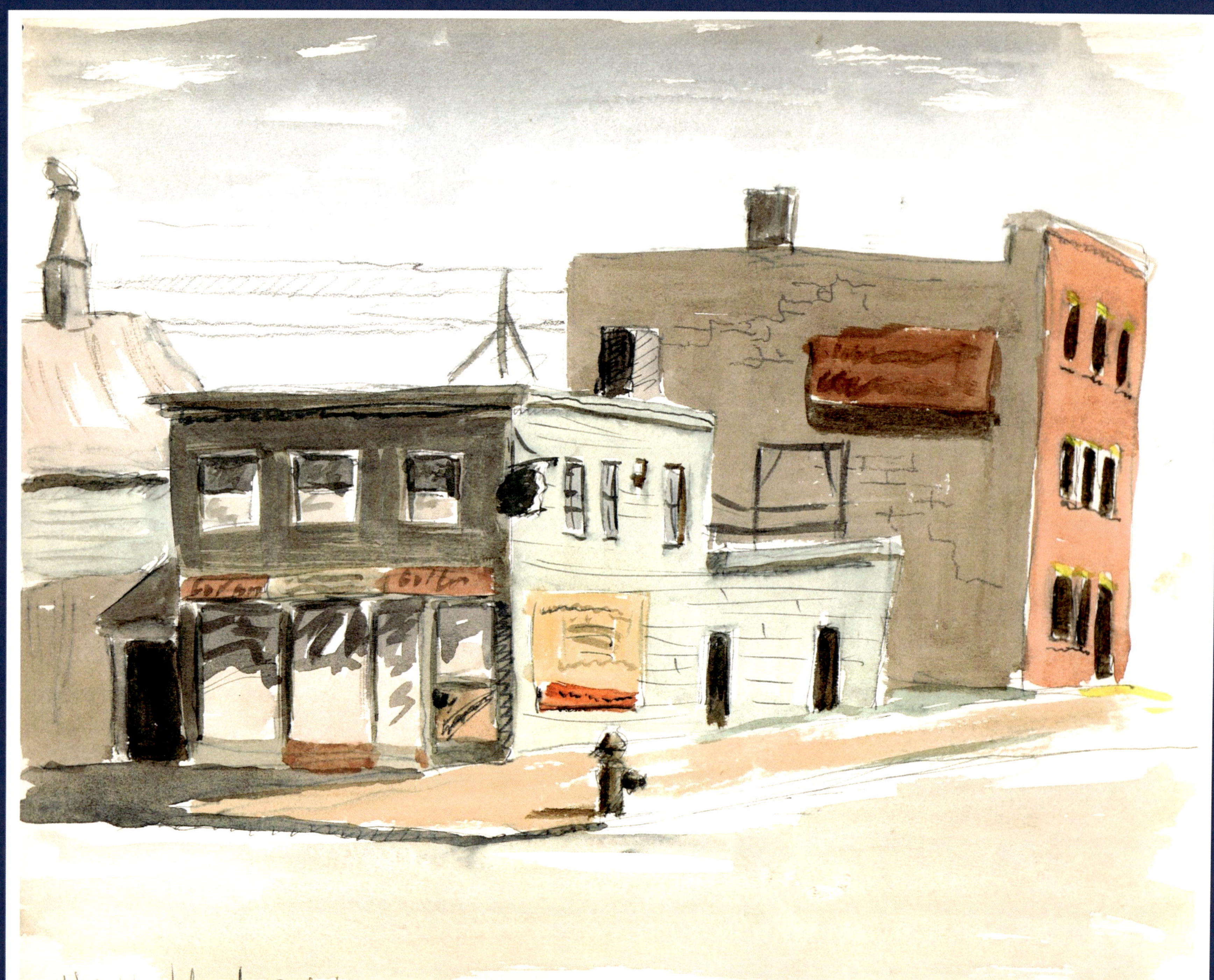

4 + Highland -Feb 43

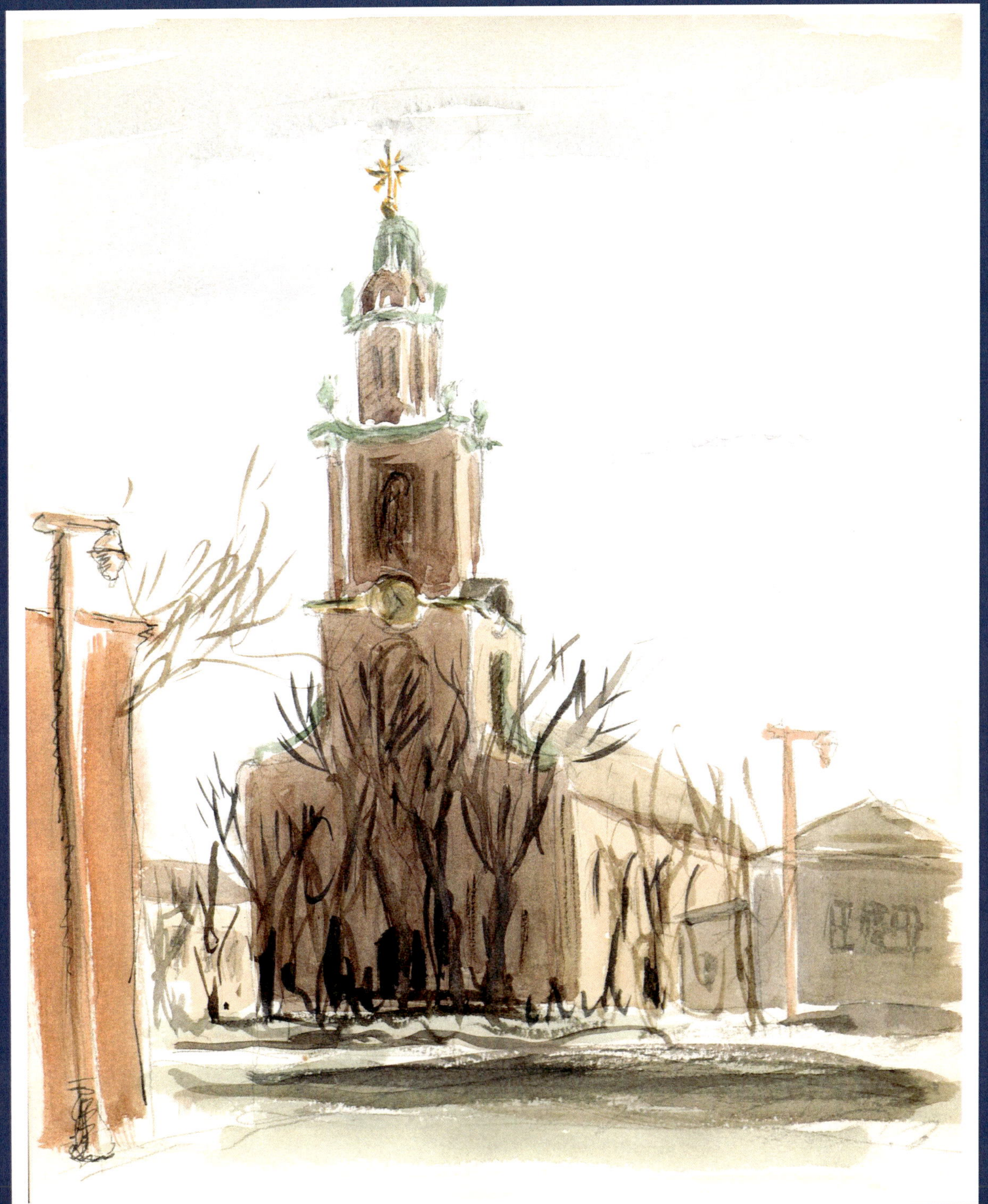

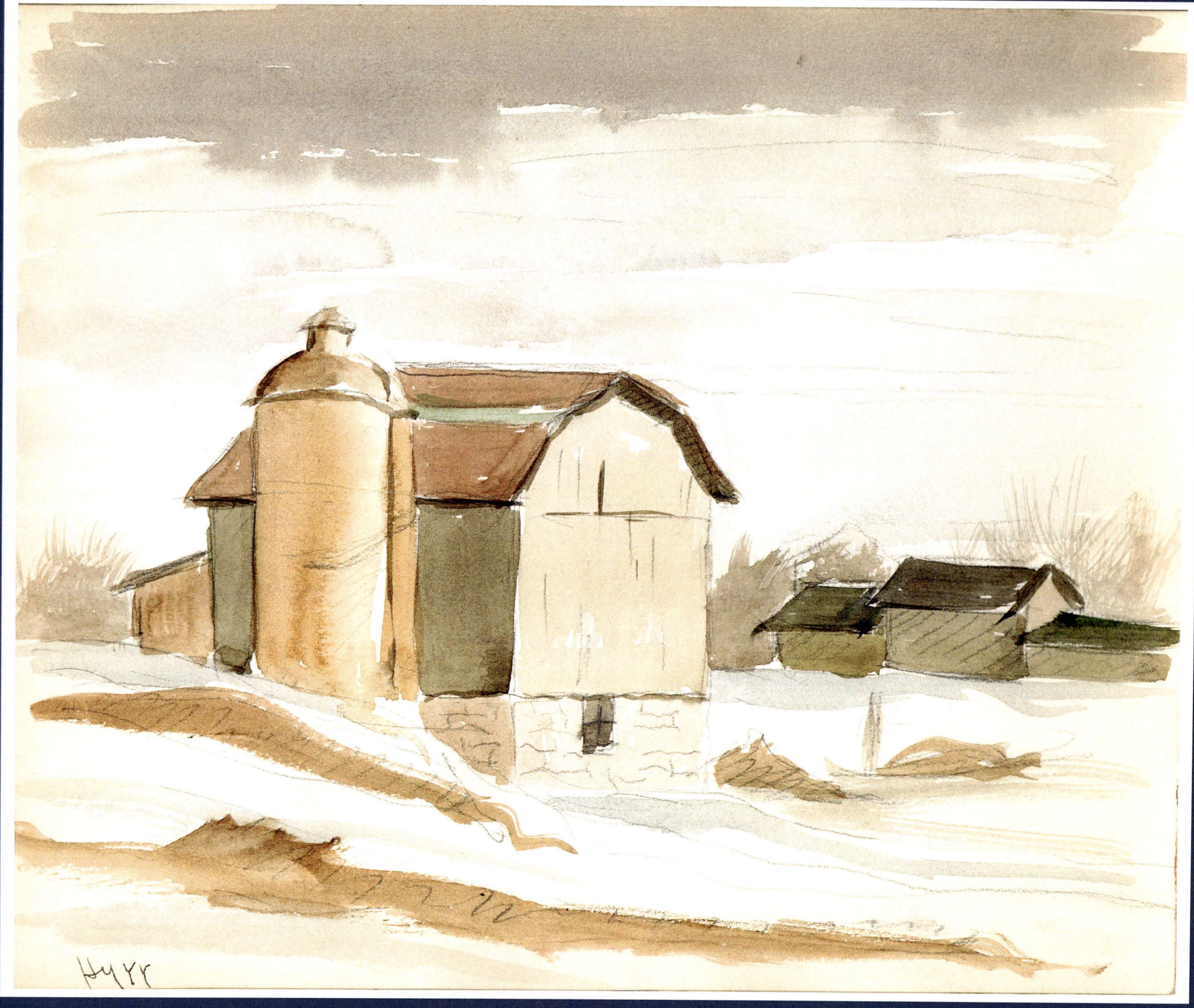

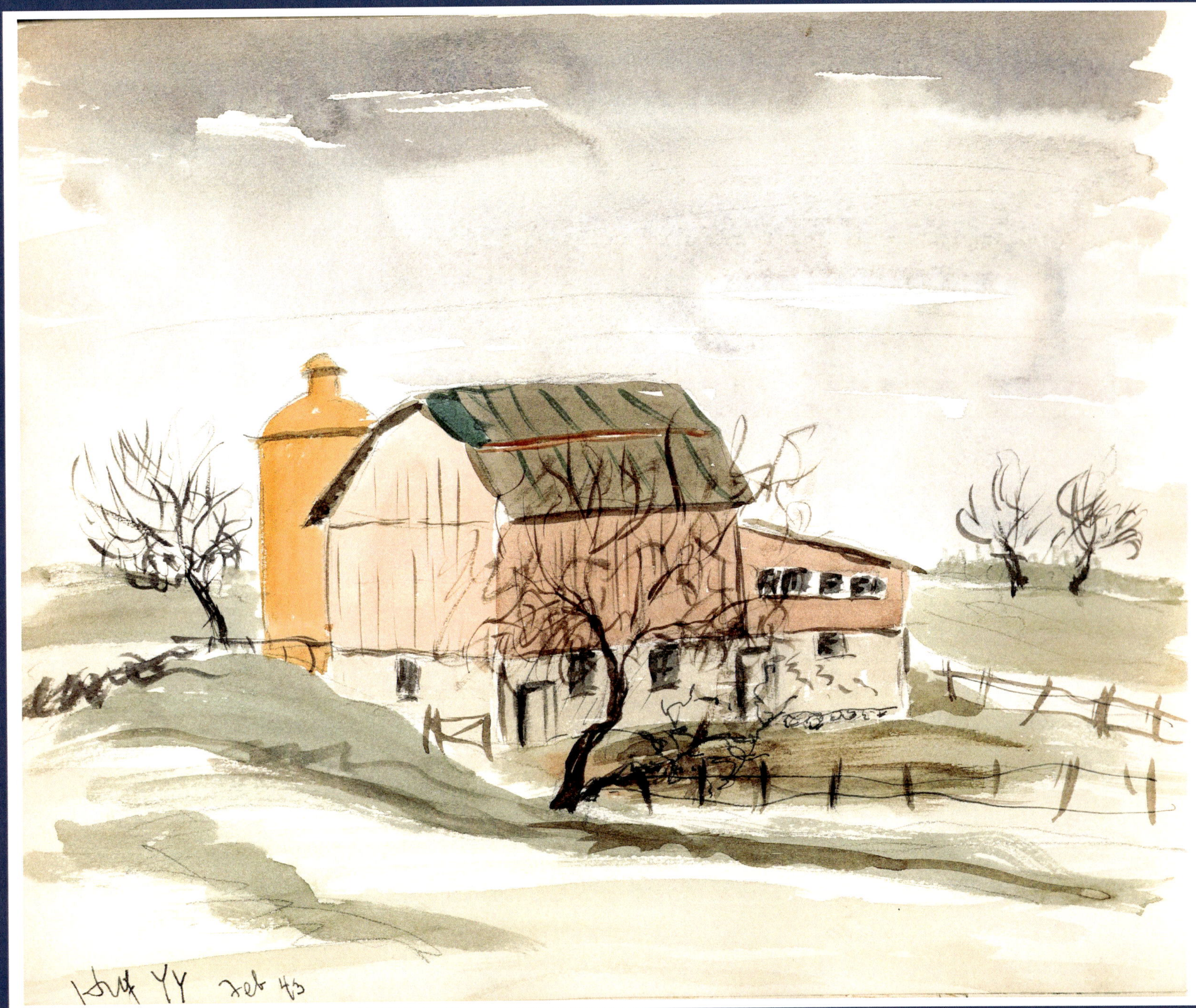

Melting snow reveals patches of bare ground in fields around faded barns.

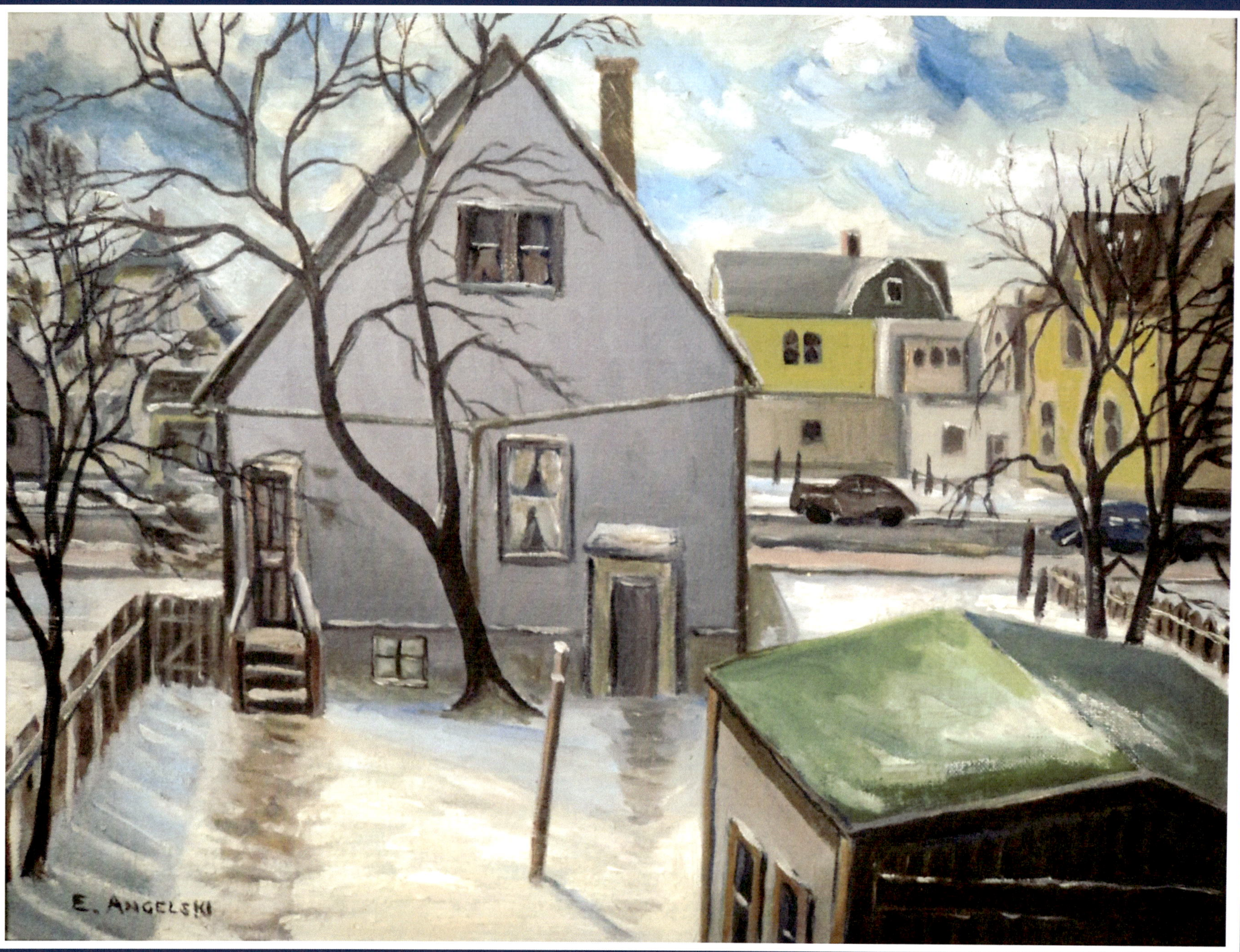
E. ANGELSKI

Wind whistles over the chimney tops
and snow-covered roofs along
residential streets.

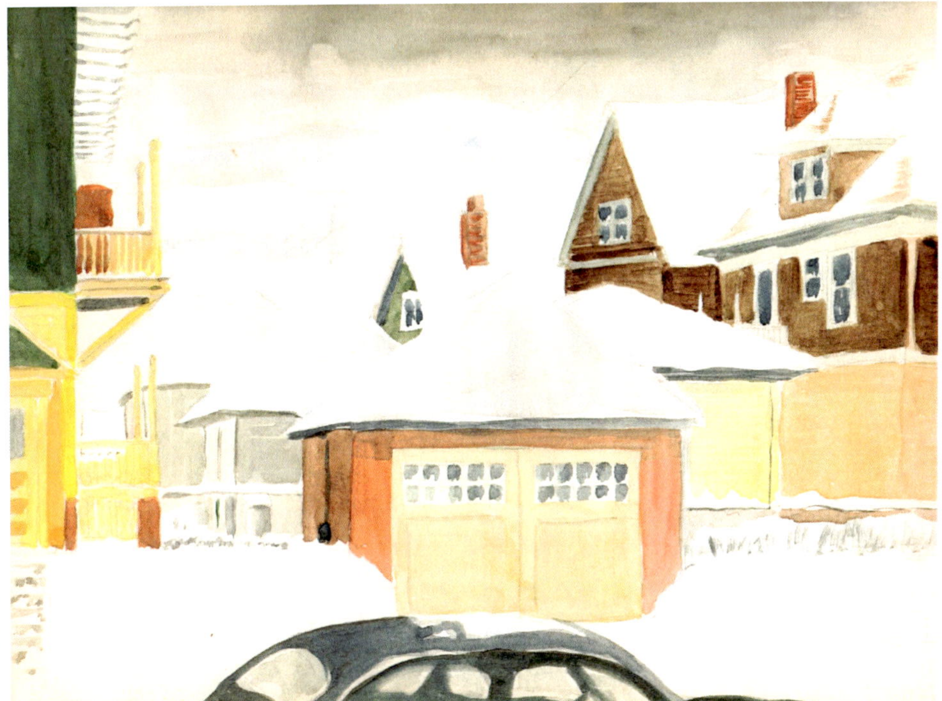



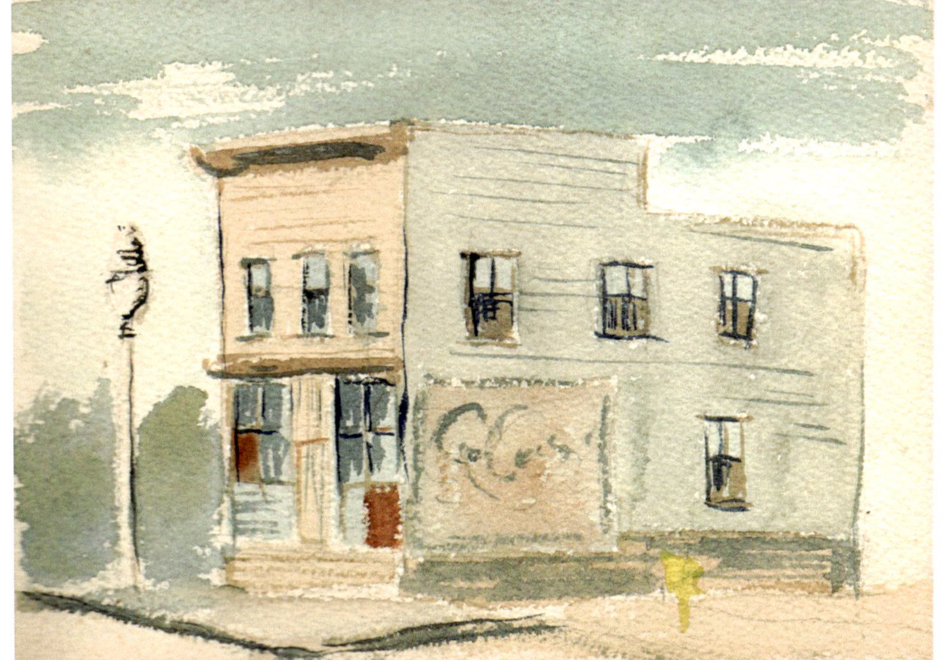

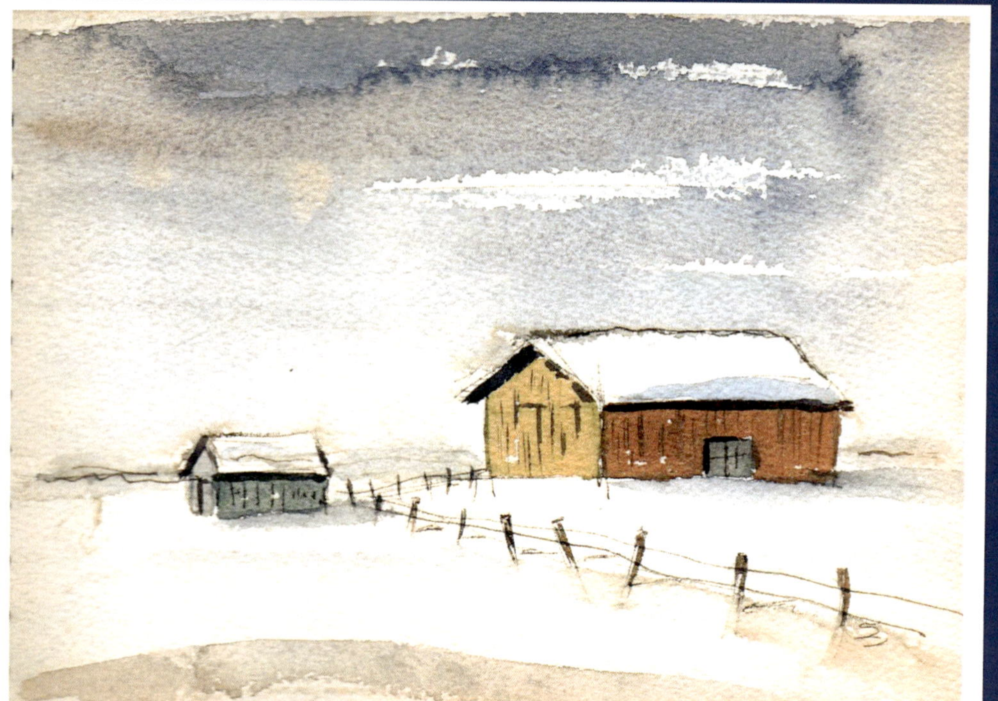

12

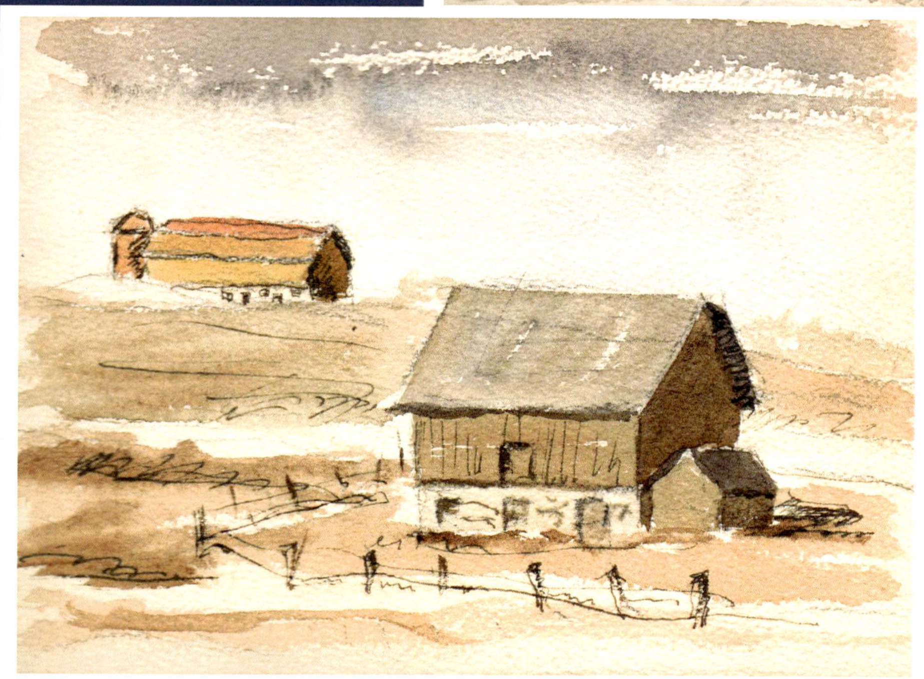

13

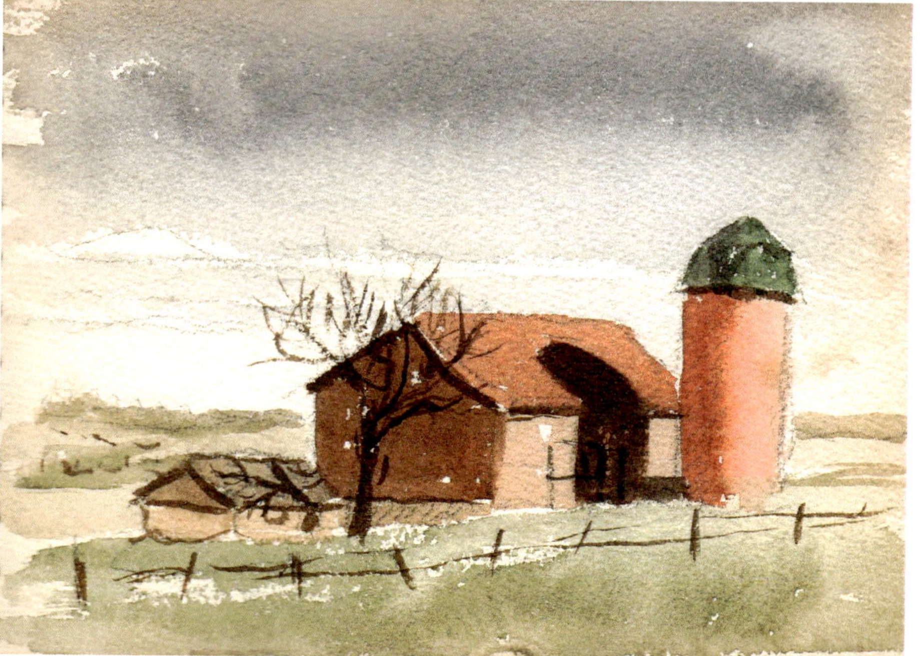

14

❖ *Now the grass, tomorrow*
*the stiff curl of wildcarrot leaf*
*One by one objects are defined —*
*It quickens: clarity, outline of leaf*

*But now the stark dignity of*
*entrance — Still, the profound change*
*has come upon them: rooted, they*
*grip down and begin to awaken*

—William Carlos Williams
"Spring and All" (excerpt)

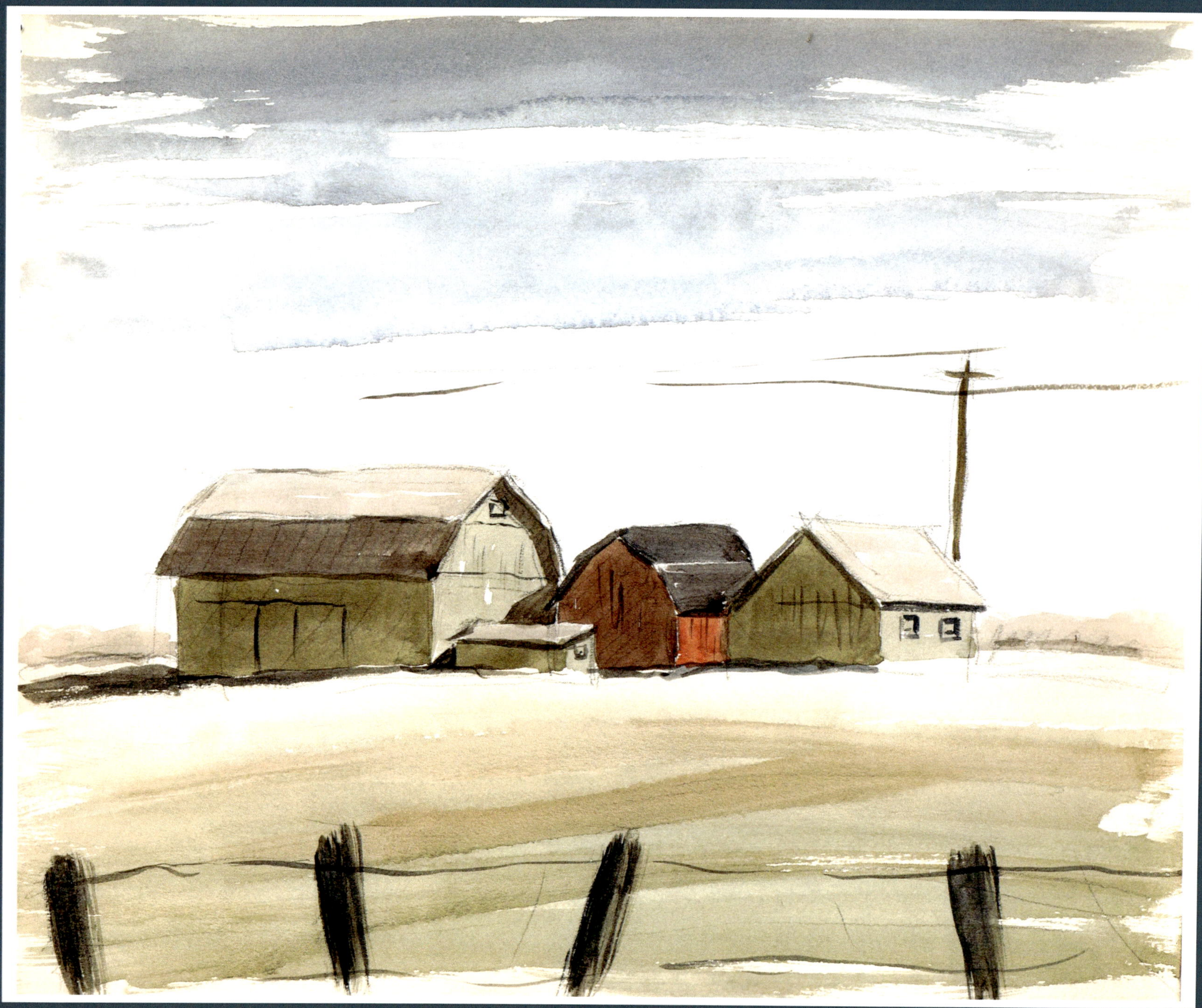

Dormant fields patiently wait for the ground to thaw.

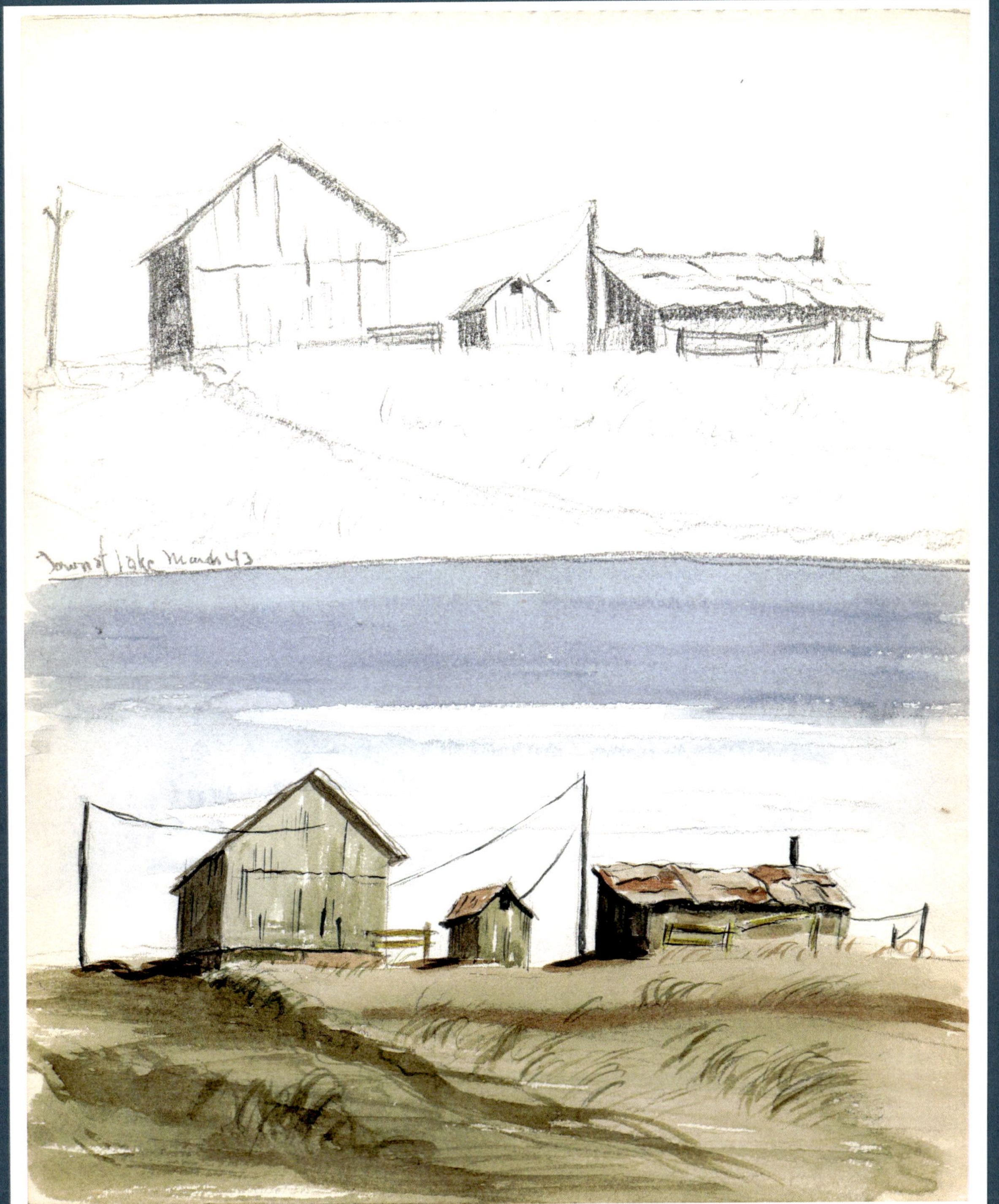

Down at Lake  March 43

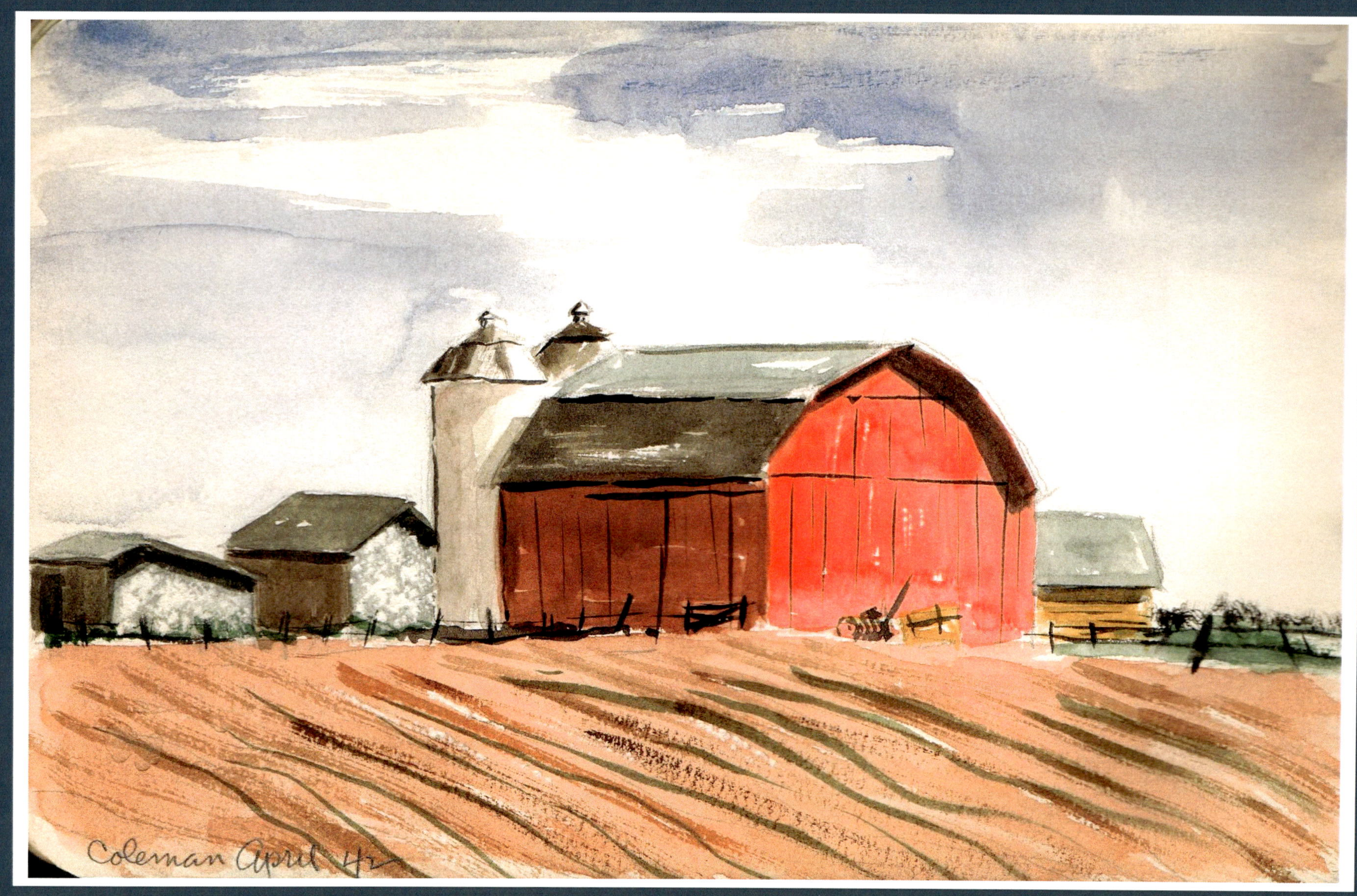

A mild day means getting the soil ready for planting.

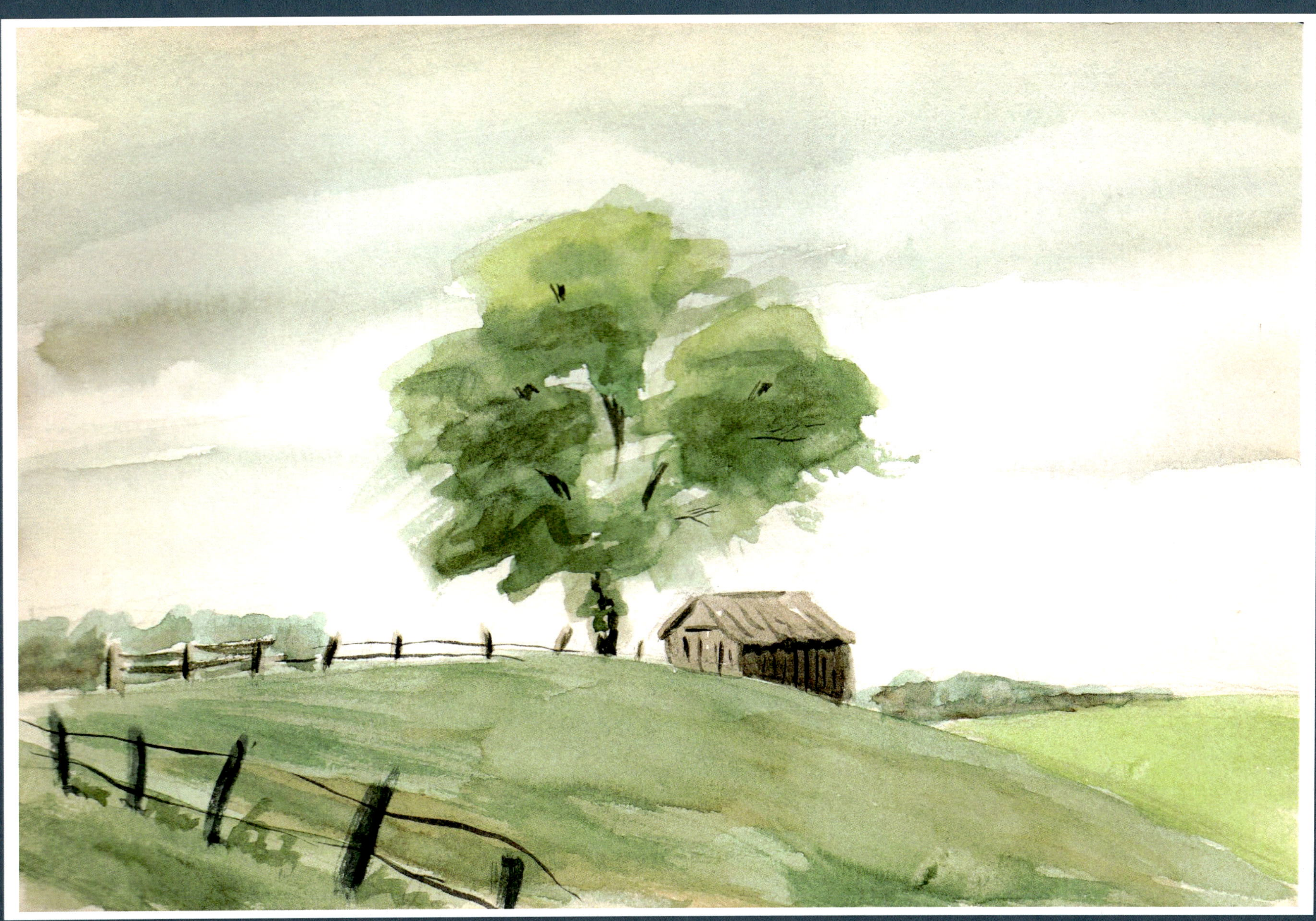

Spring showers awaken the grasses, and buds turn into leaves on a solitary tree on the hill.

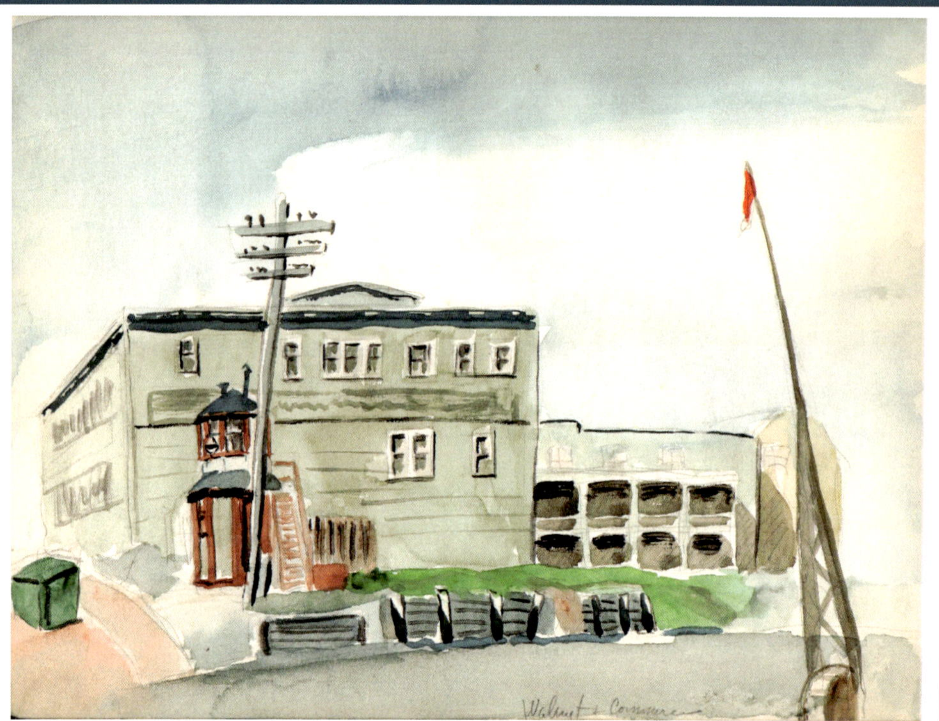
Walnut & Commerce



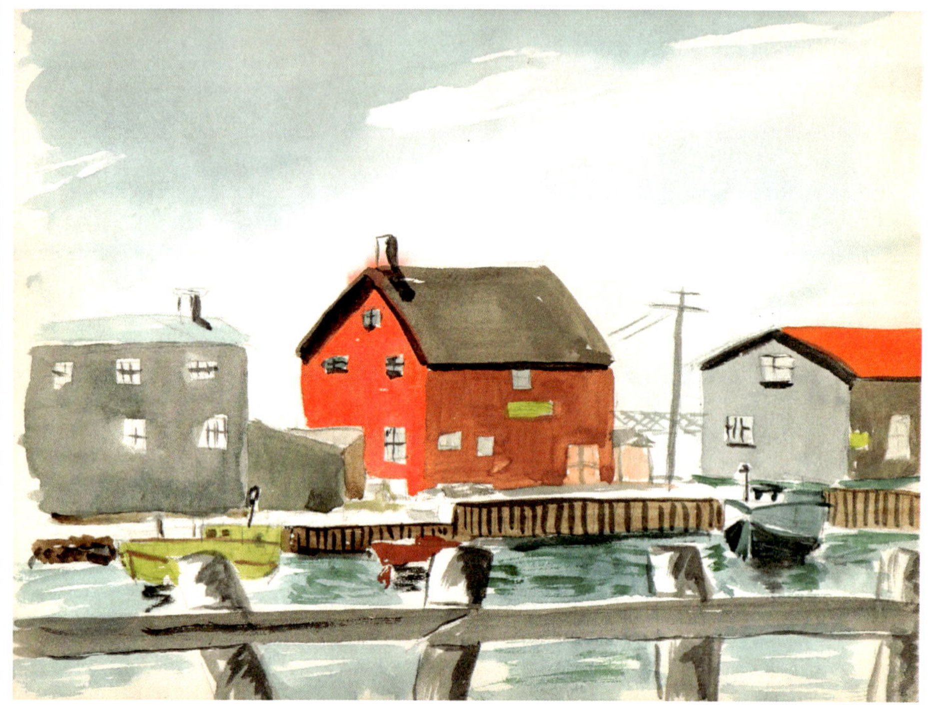

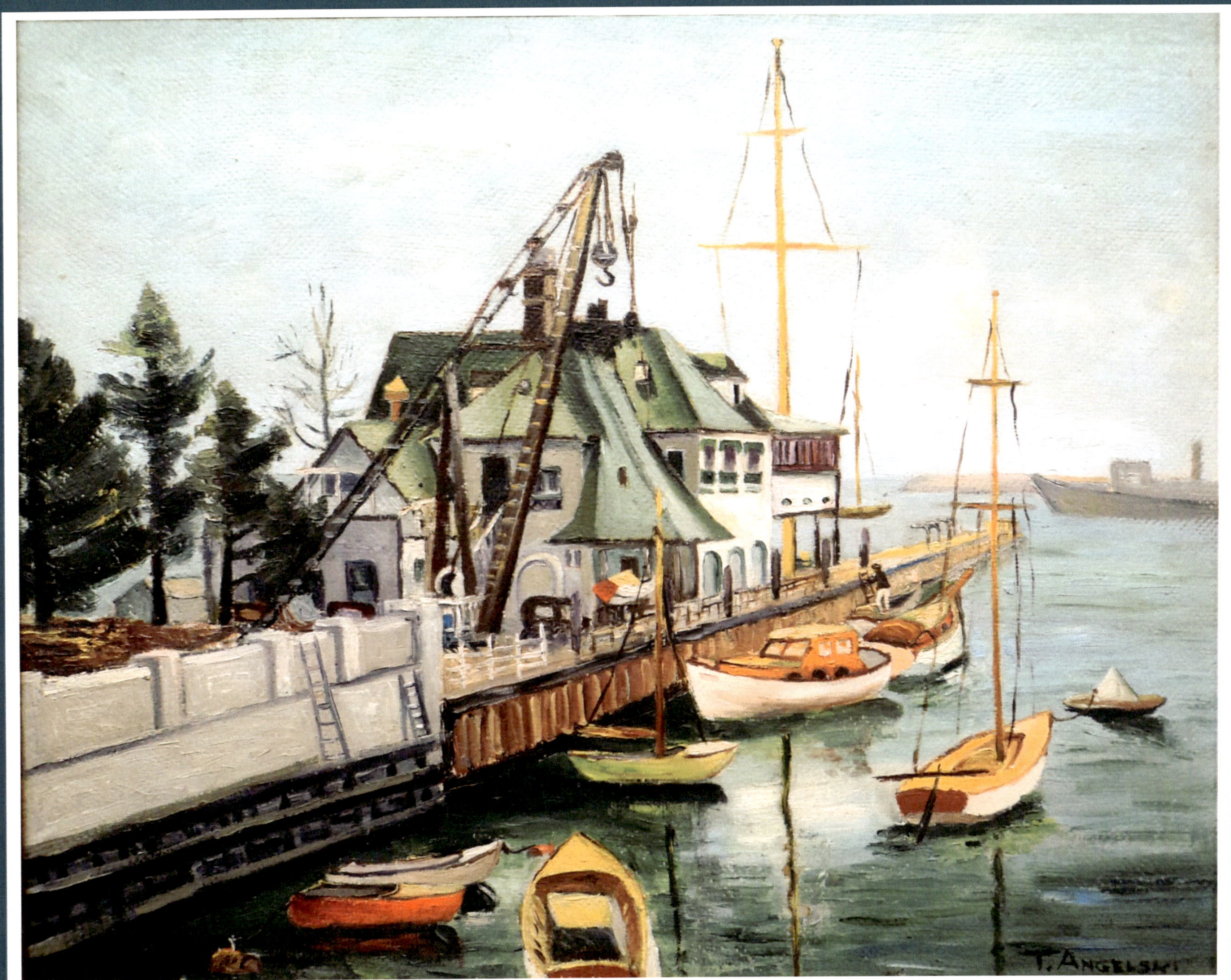

As a slight haze hangs over the lake, boats are lowered gently into the water.

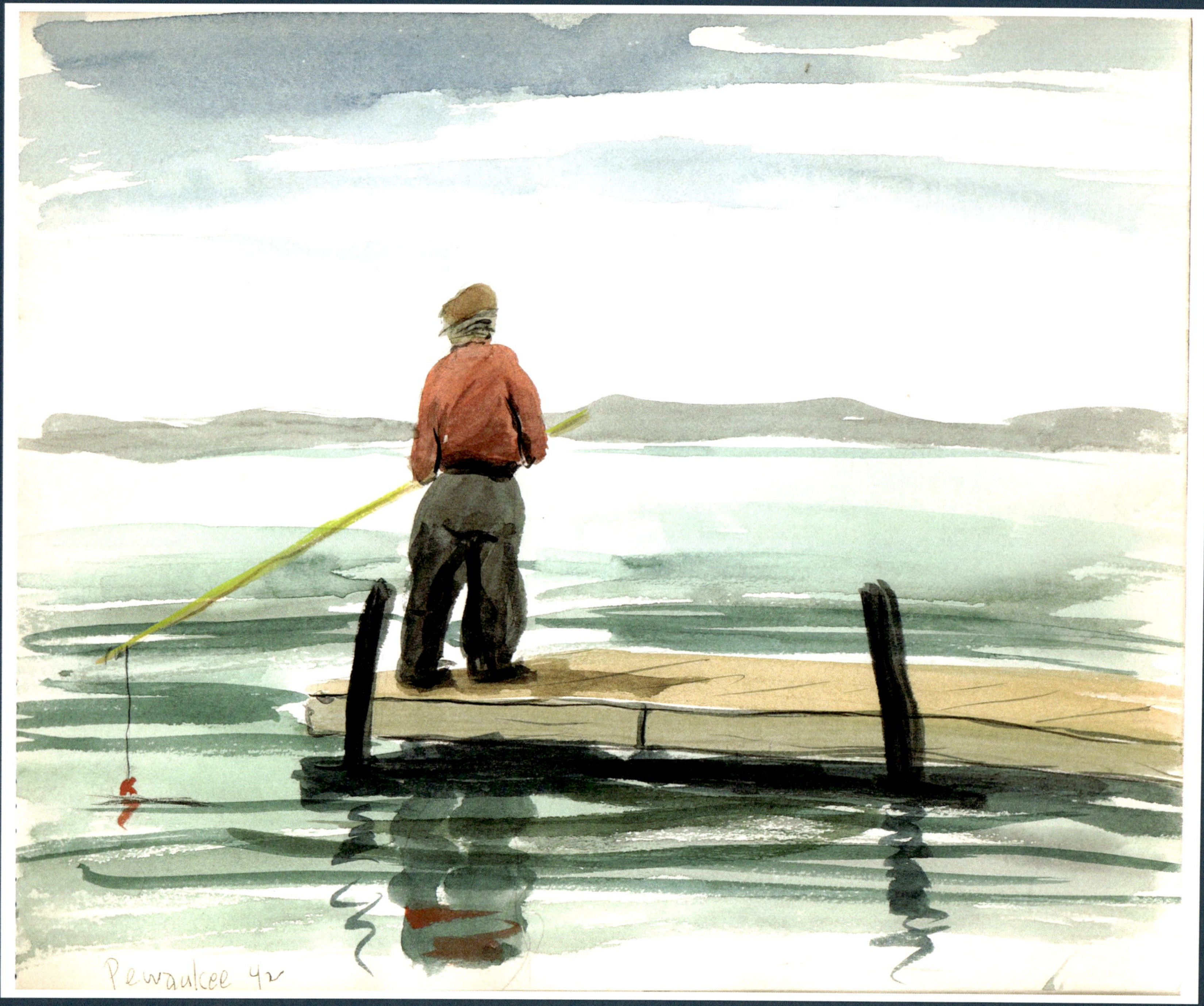




Inland lakes welcome the return of fishermen and boaters enjoying a leisurely morning.

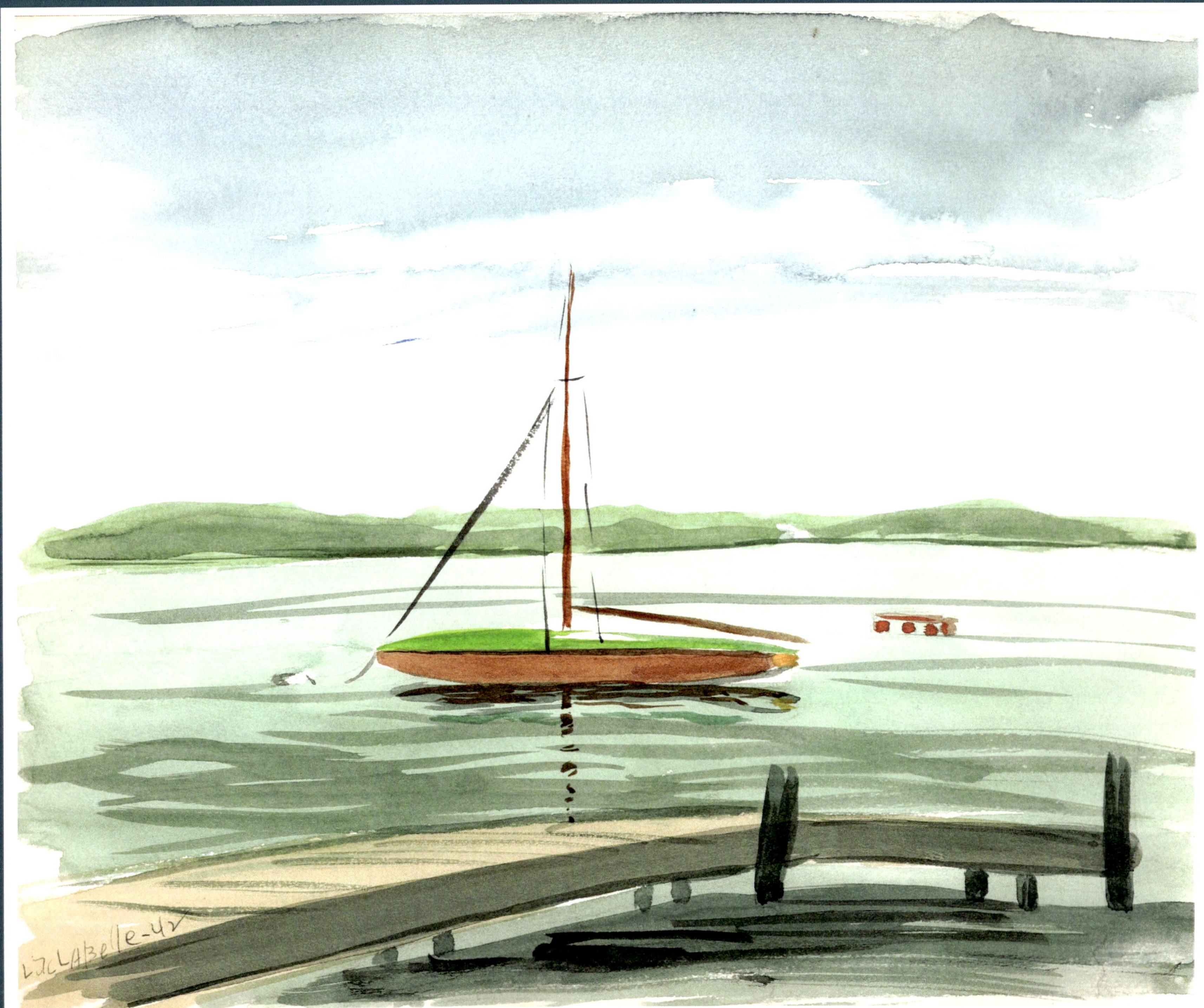
LacLaBelle-42

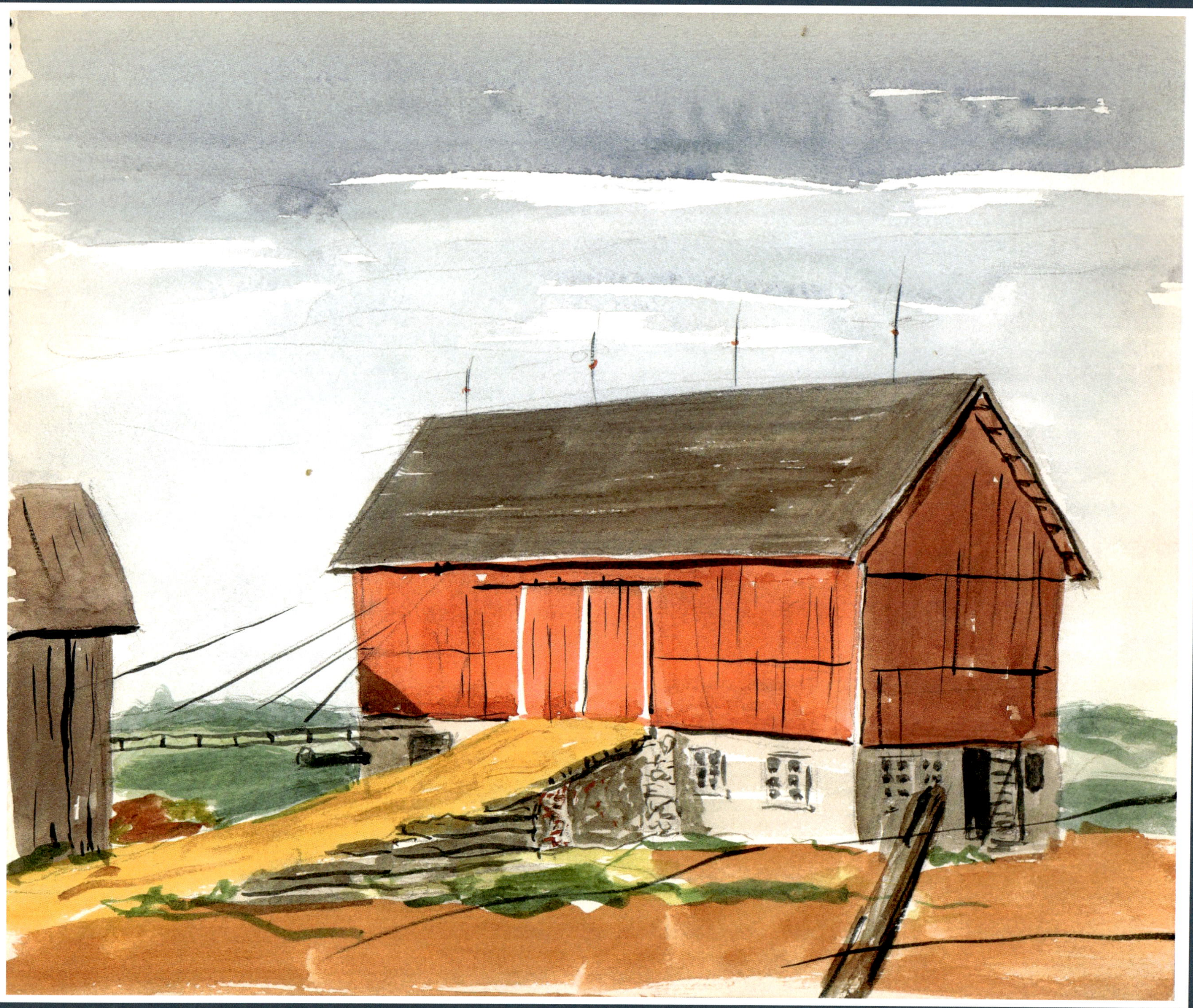

❖ *When summer time has come, and all*
*The world is in the magic thrall*
*Of perfumed airs that lull each sense*
*To fits of drowsy indolence;*
*When skies are deepest blue above,*
*And flow'rs aflush,—then most I love*
*To start, while early dews are damp,*
*And wend my way in woodland tramp*
*Where forests rustle, tree on tree,*
*And sing their silent songs to me;*
*Where pathways meet and pathways part,—*
*To walk with Nature heart by heart,*
*Till wearied out at last I lie*
*Where some sweet stream steals singing by*
*A mossy bank; where violets vie*
*In color with the summer sky,—*

—Paul Laurence Dunbar
"In Summer Time" (excerpt)

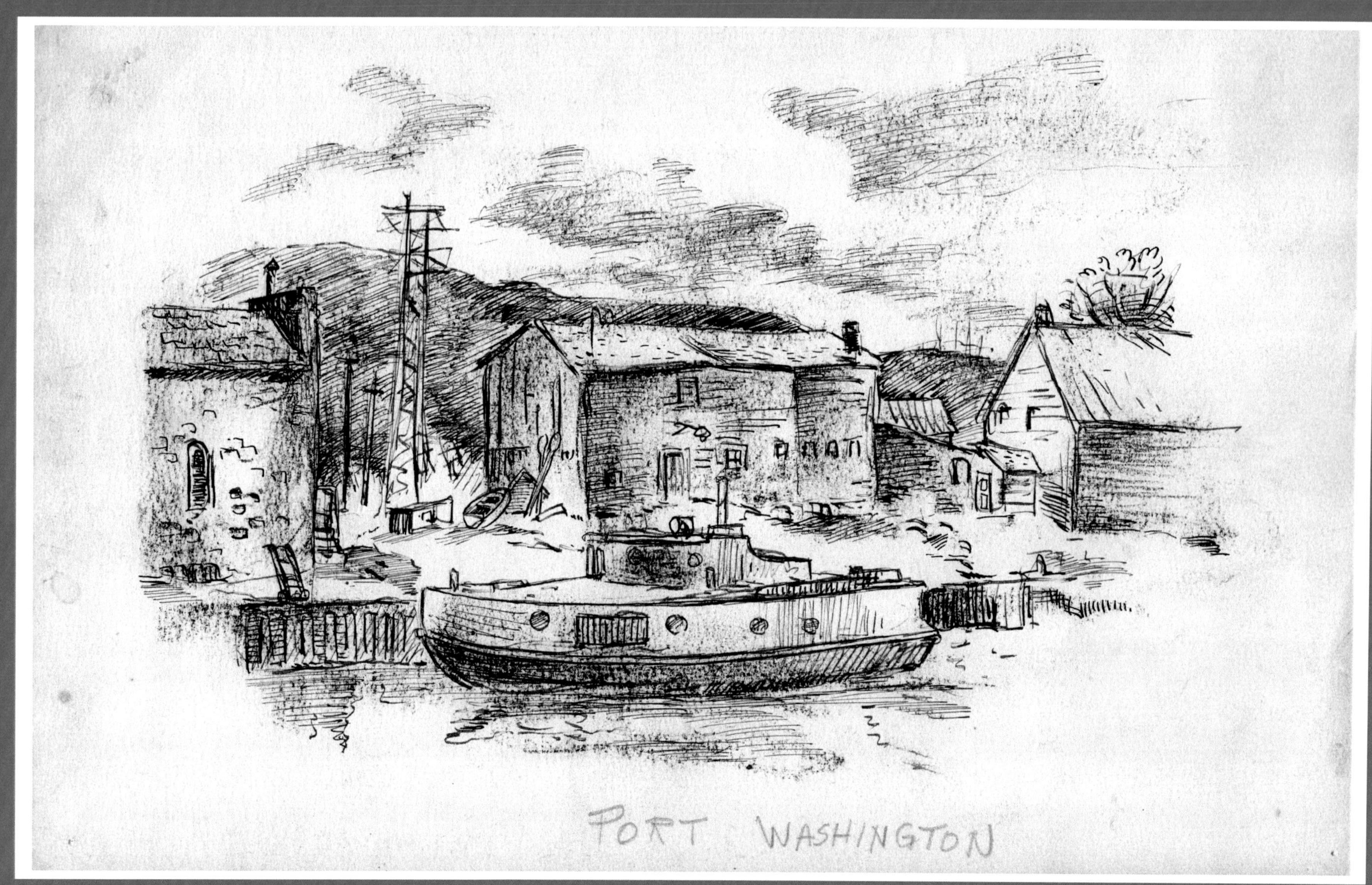
PORT WASHINGTON

The lake breeze is especially inviting on one of the first hot days of summer.

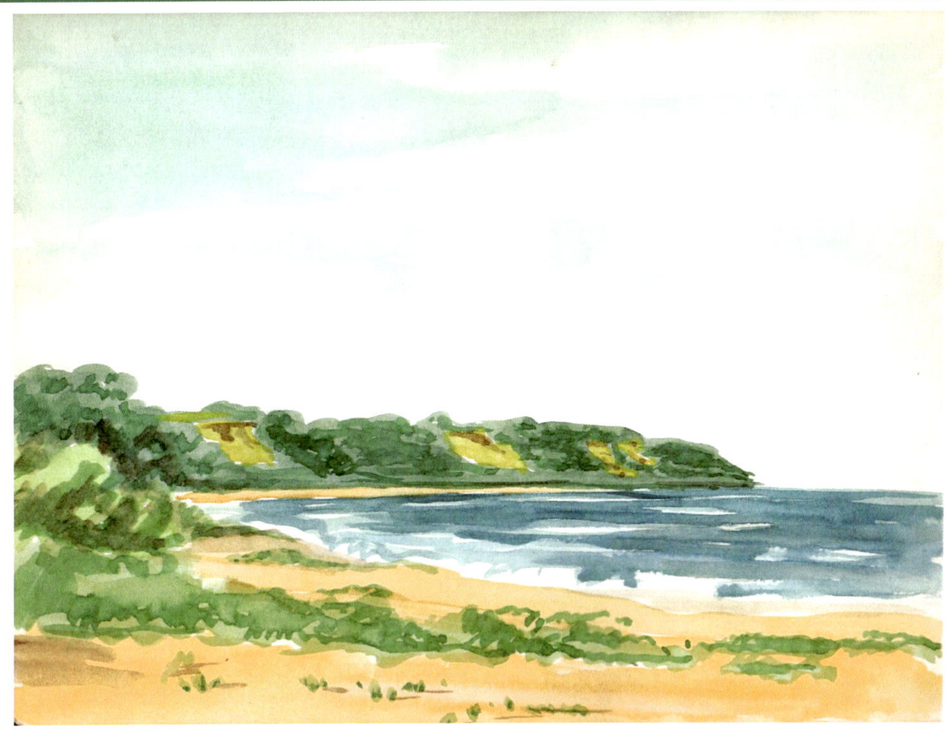



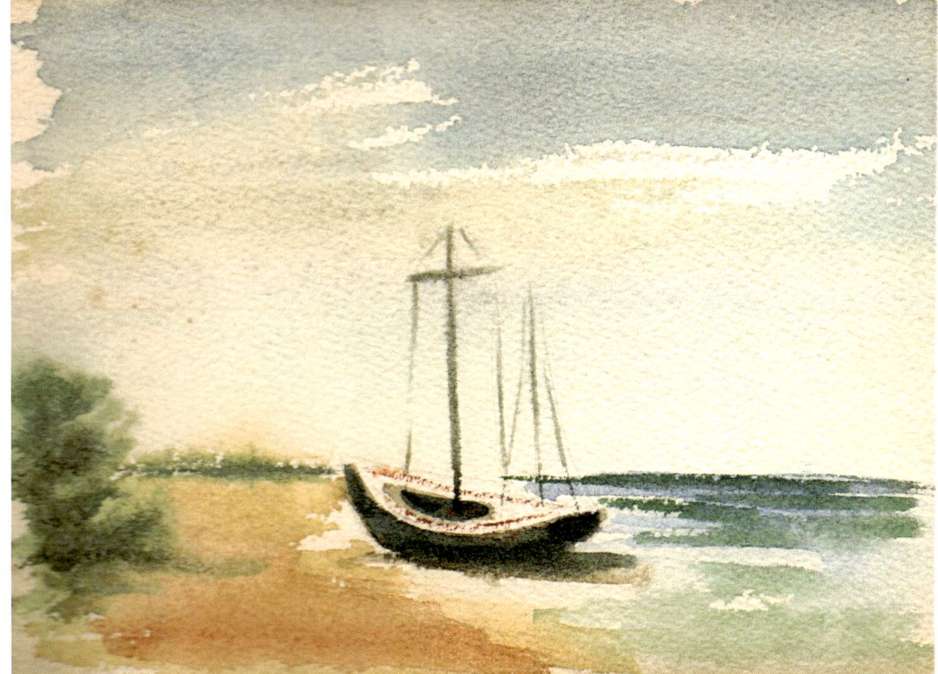

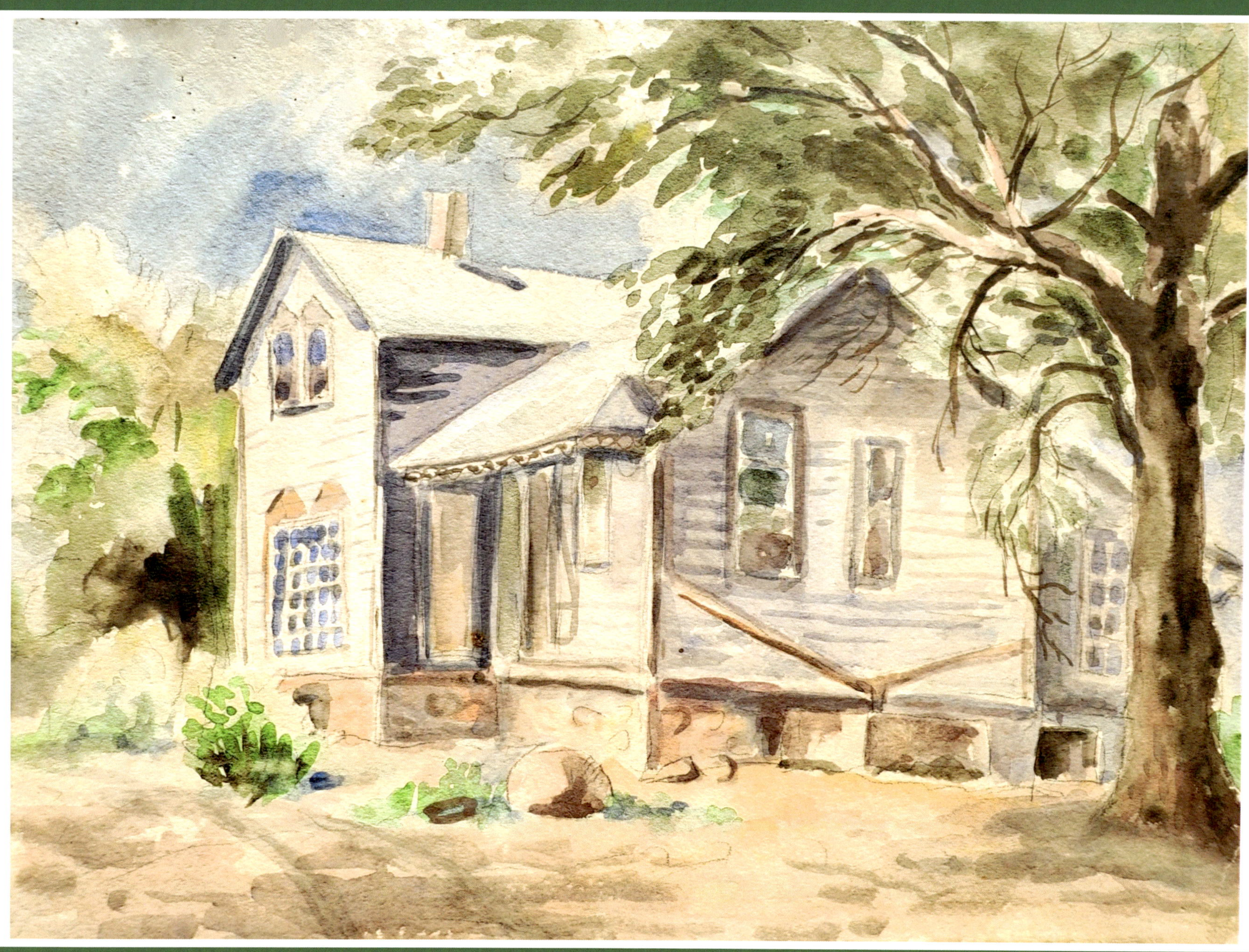

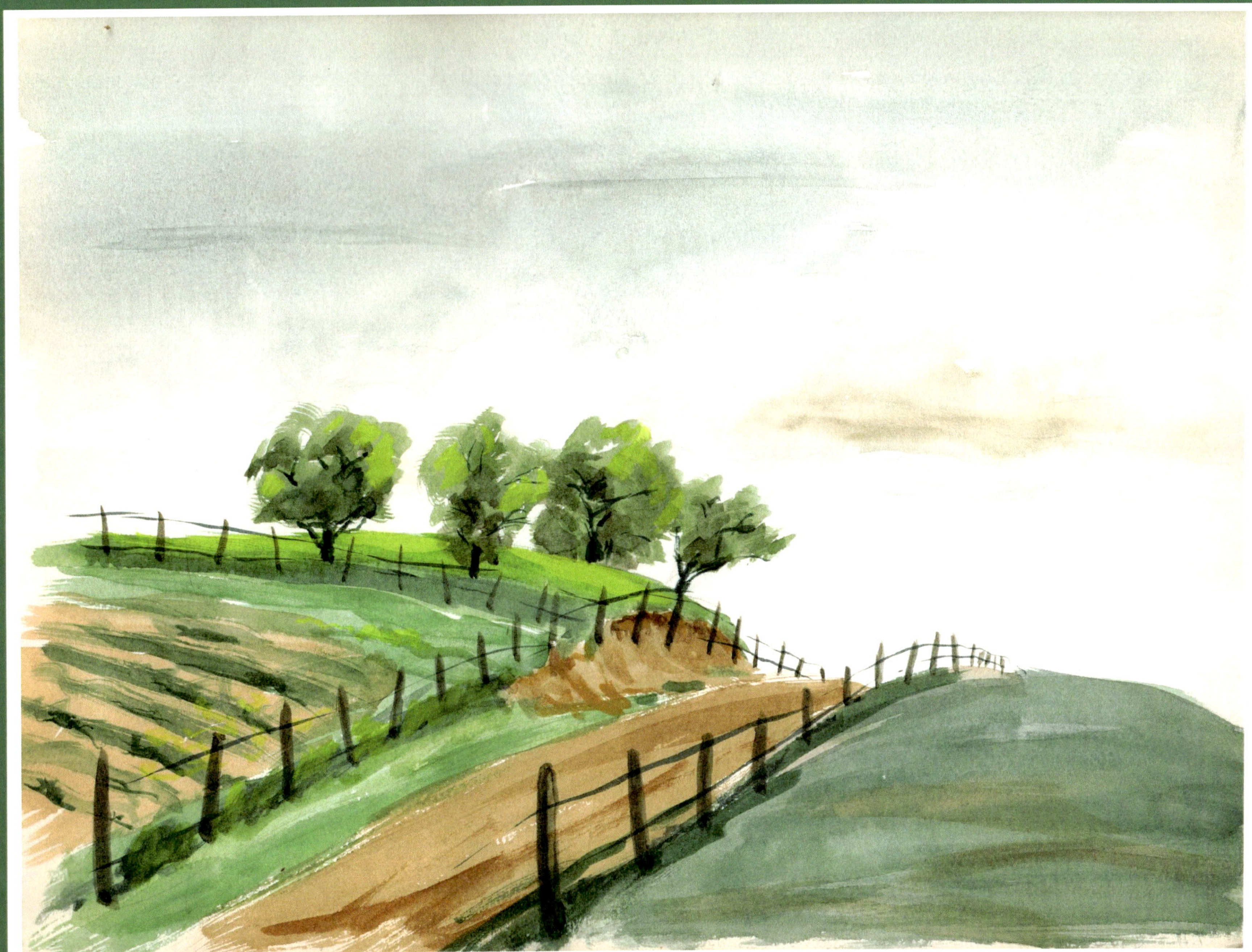

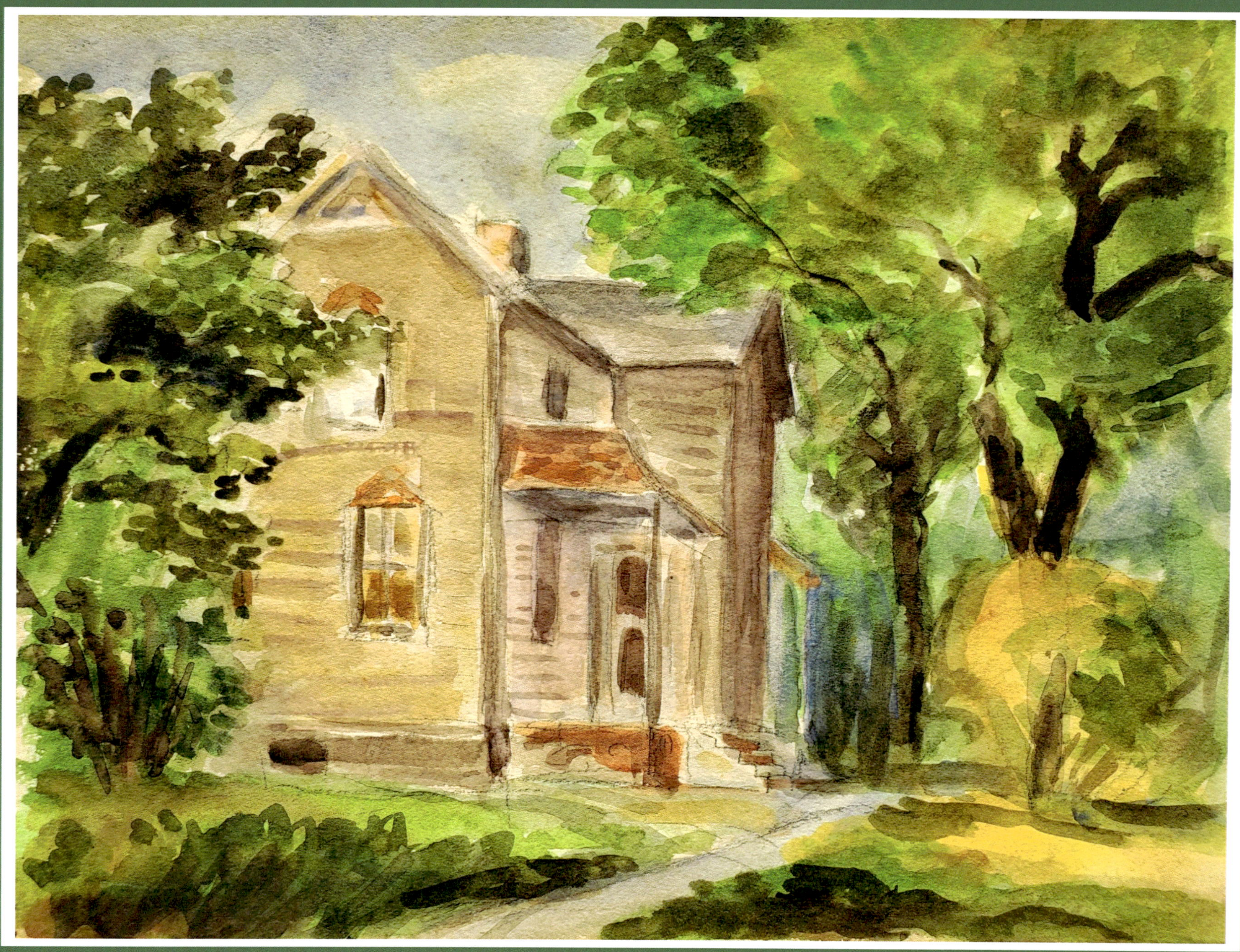

Greenery flourishes around an old farmhouse and barn.

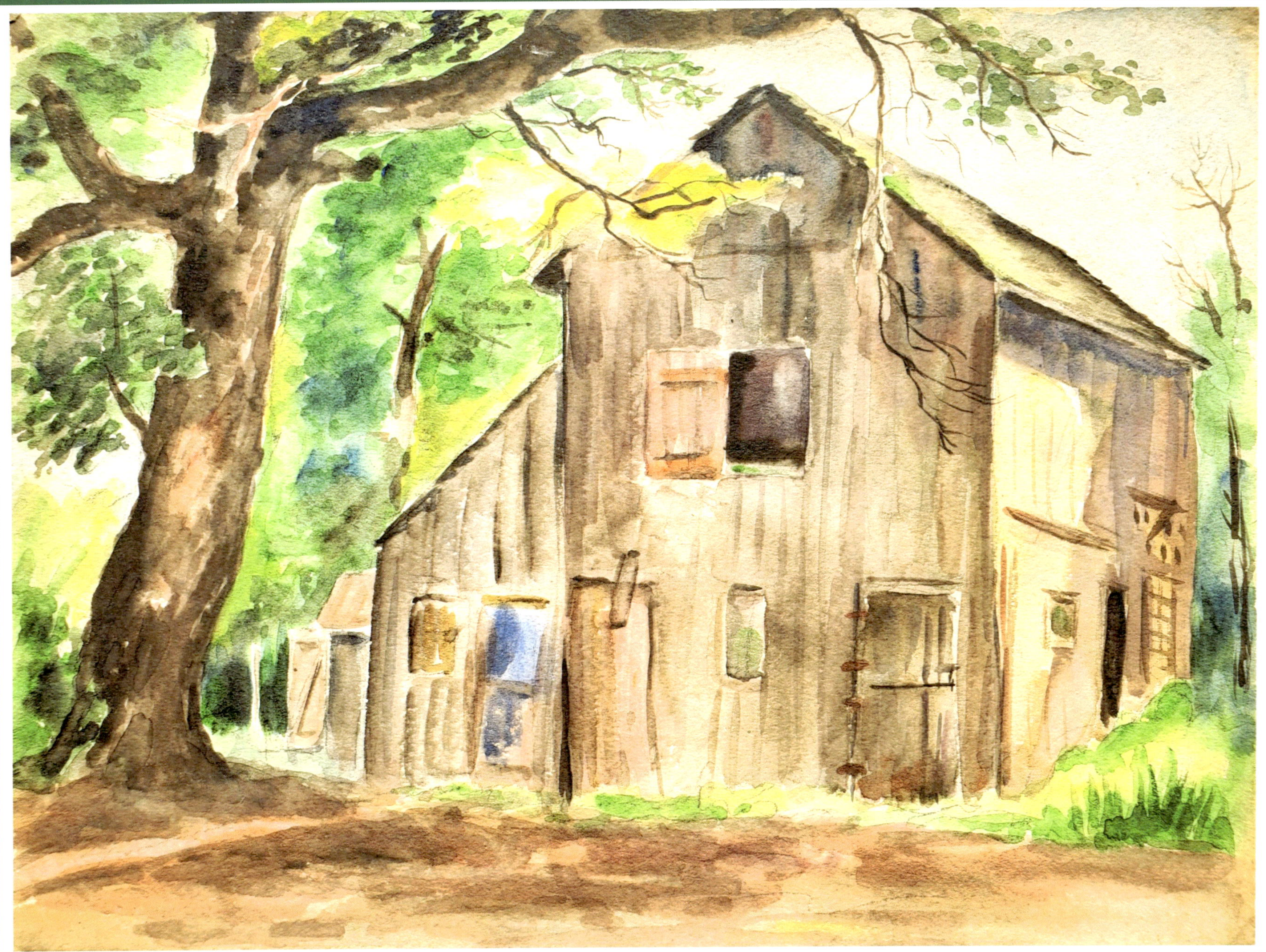

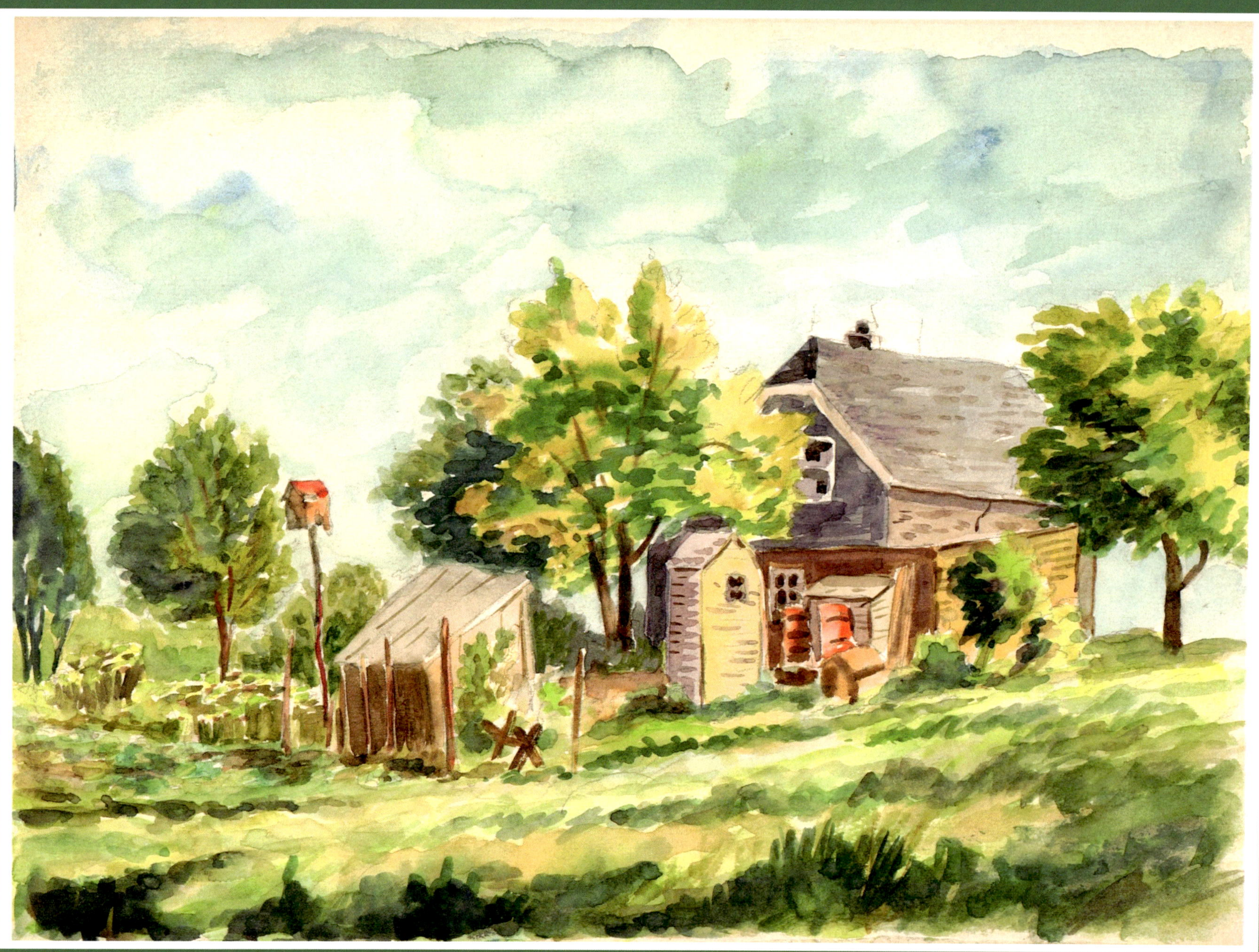

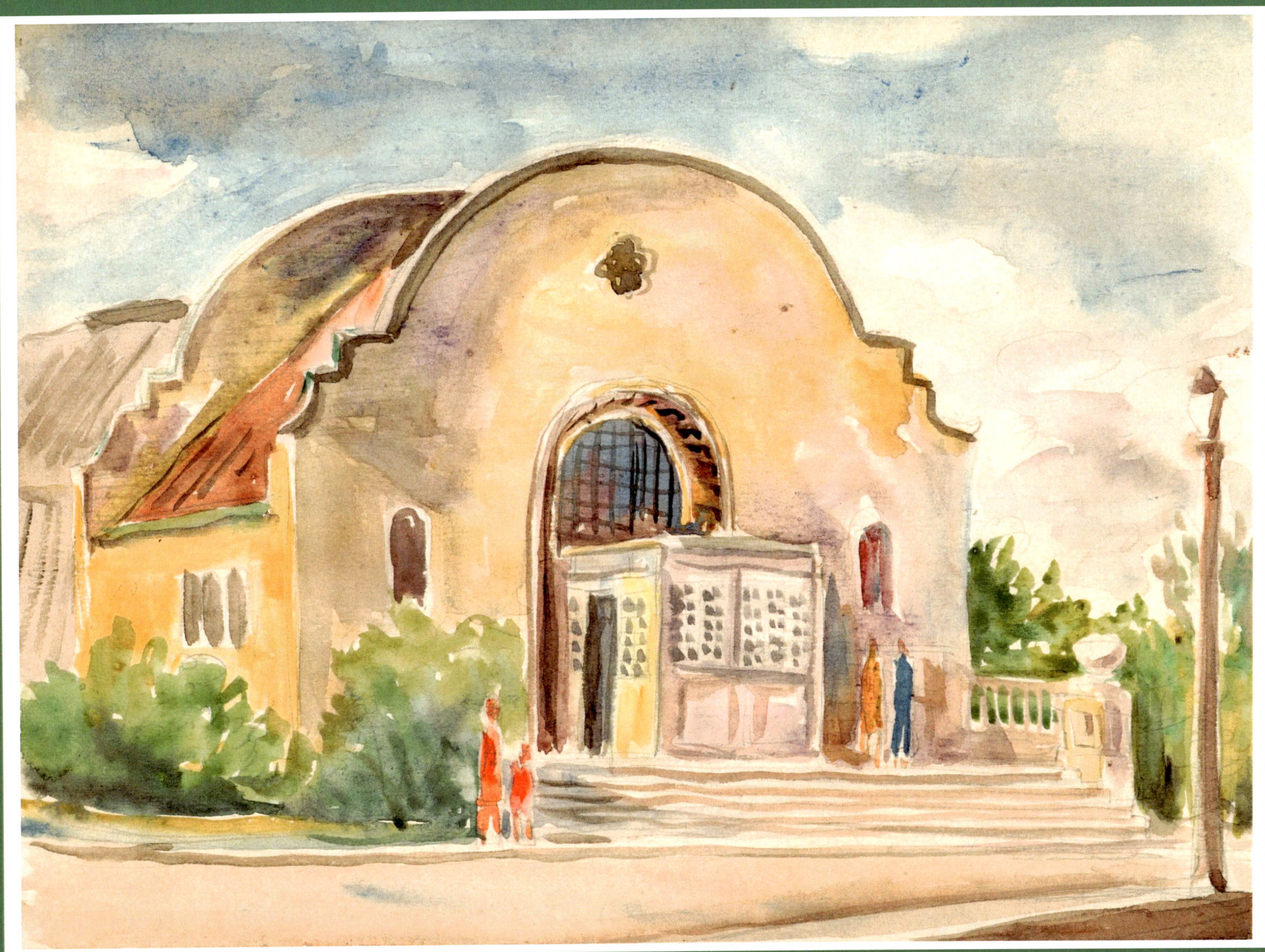

It is the perfect afternoon for a stroll through one of the neighborhood parks.

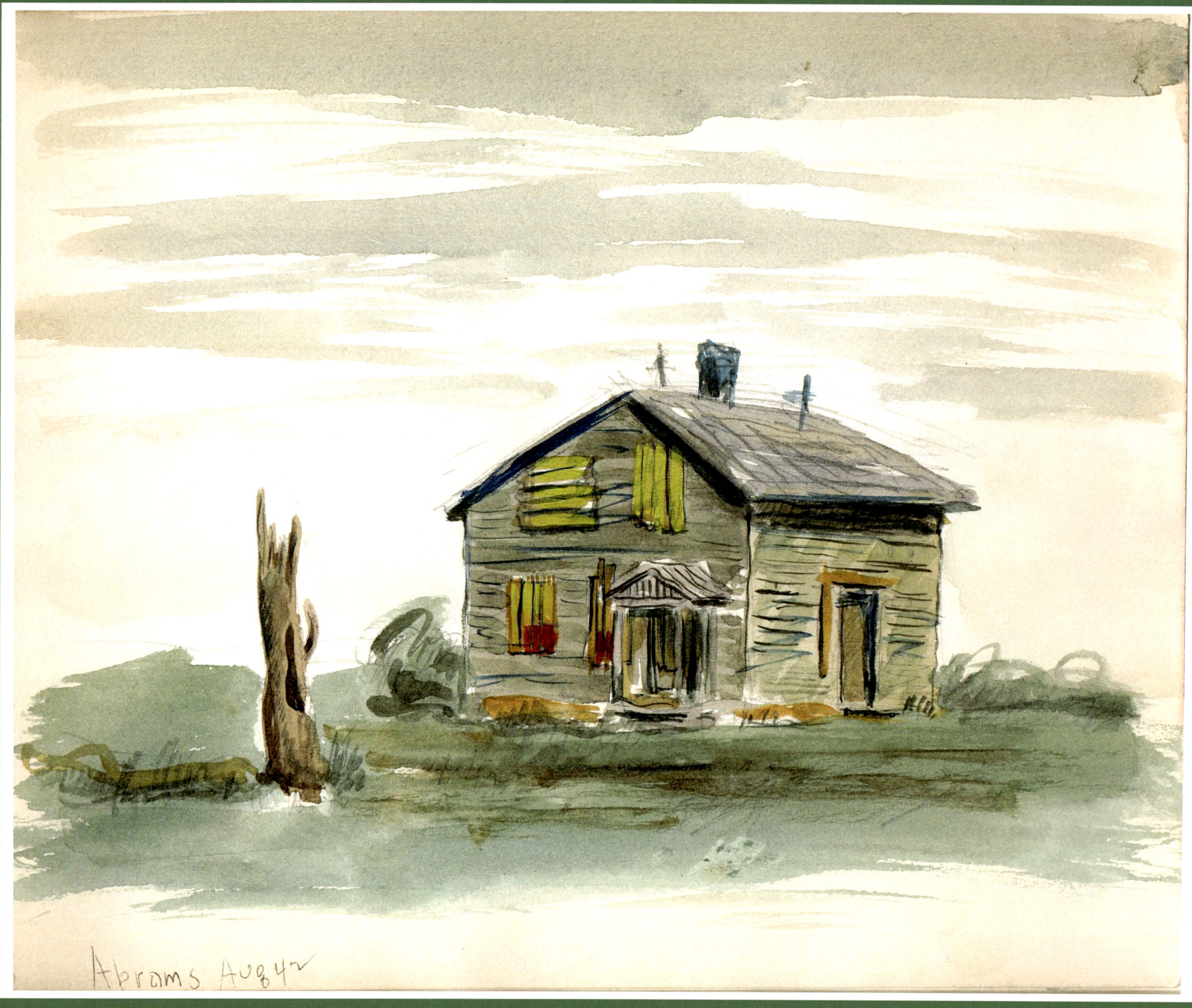

Abrams Aug 42

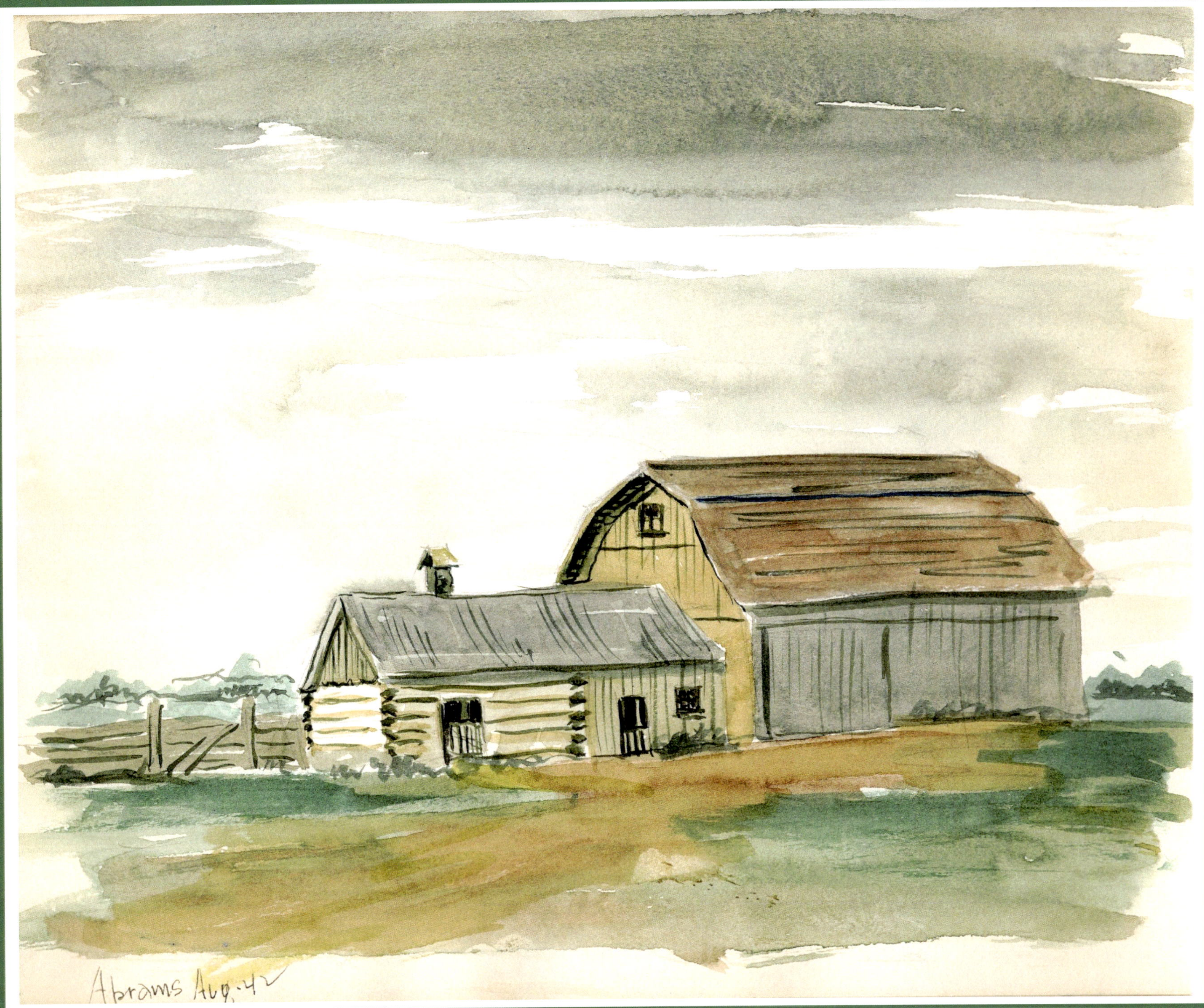
Abrams Aug. 42

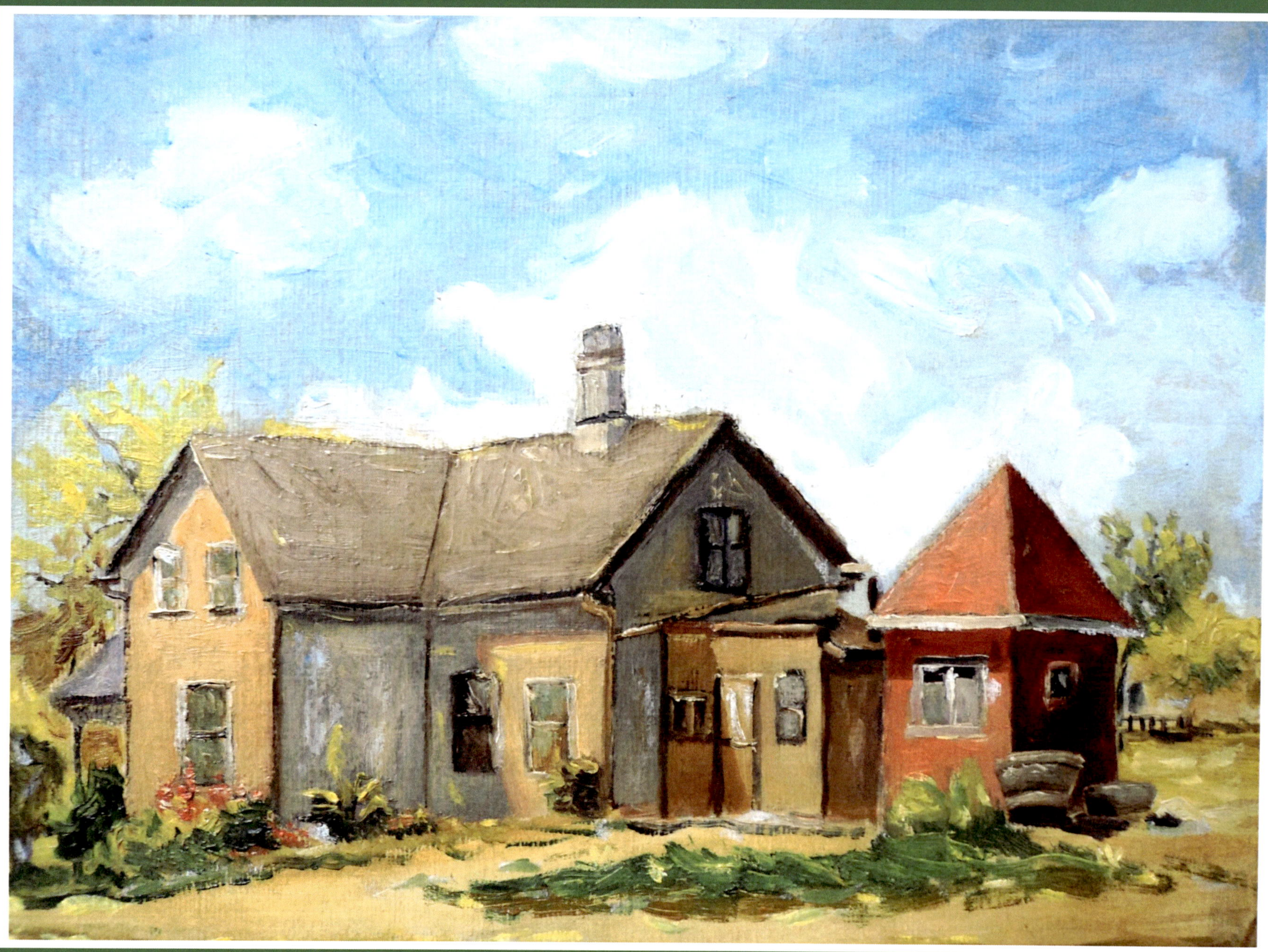

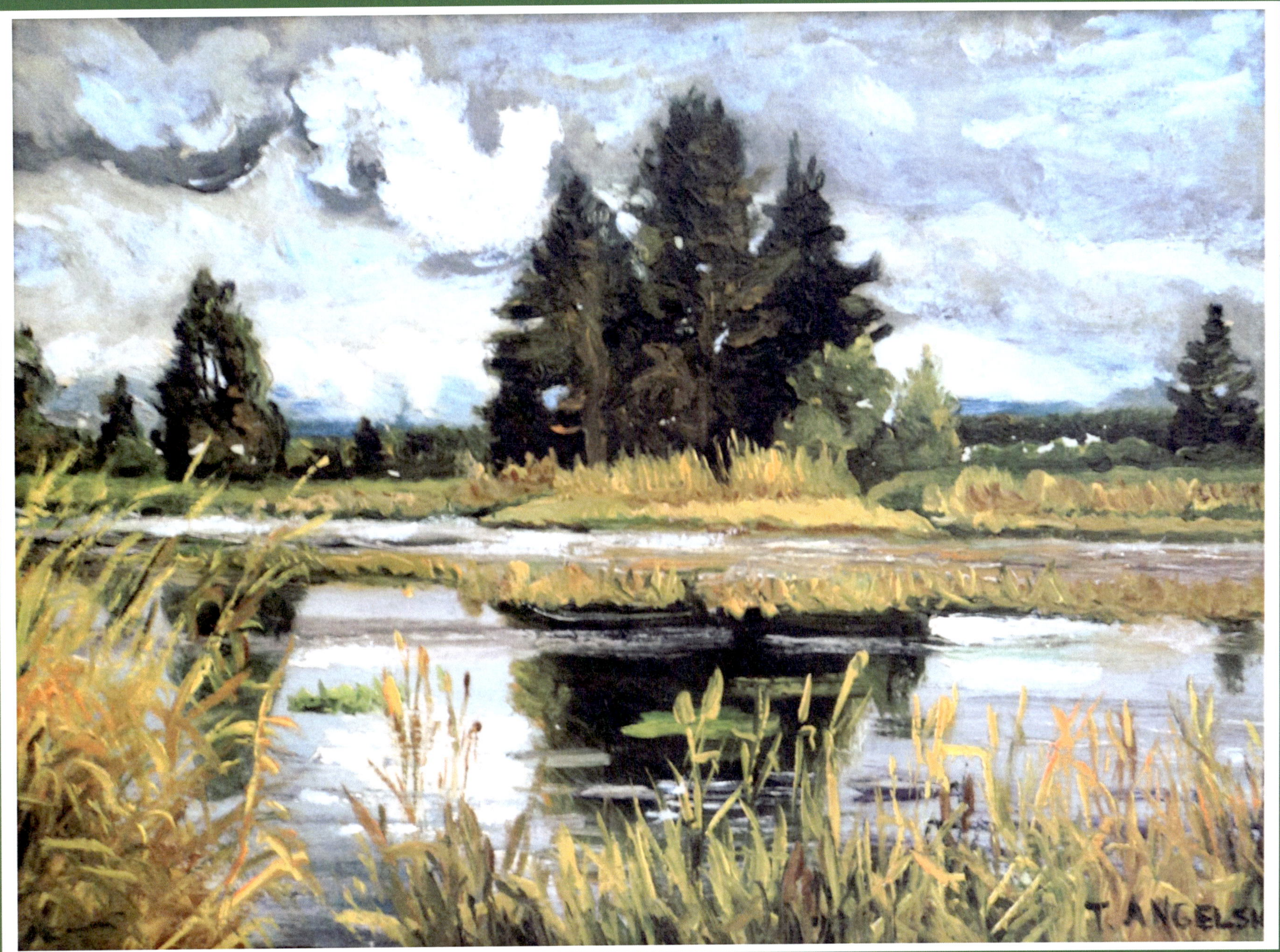

Strong thunderstorms darken the sky and saturate the wetlands.

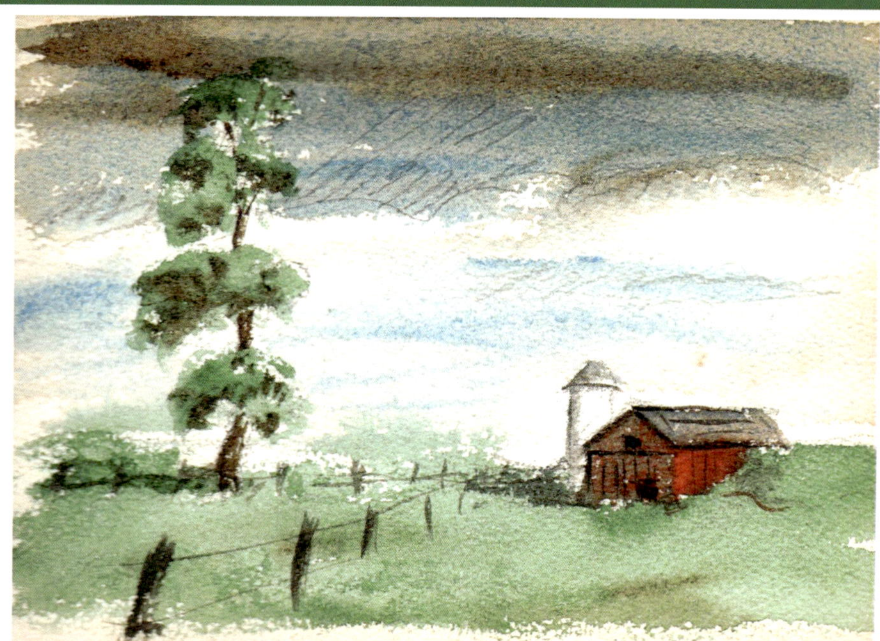

38

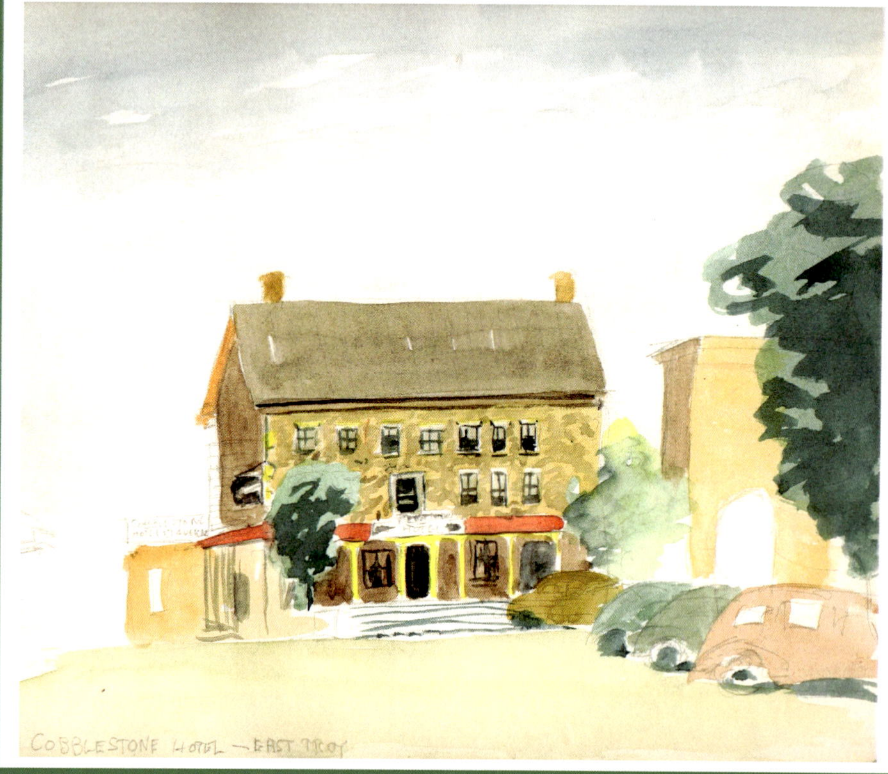


39

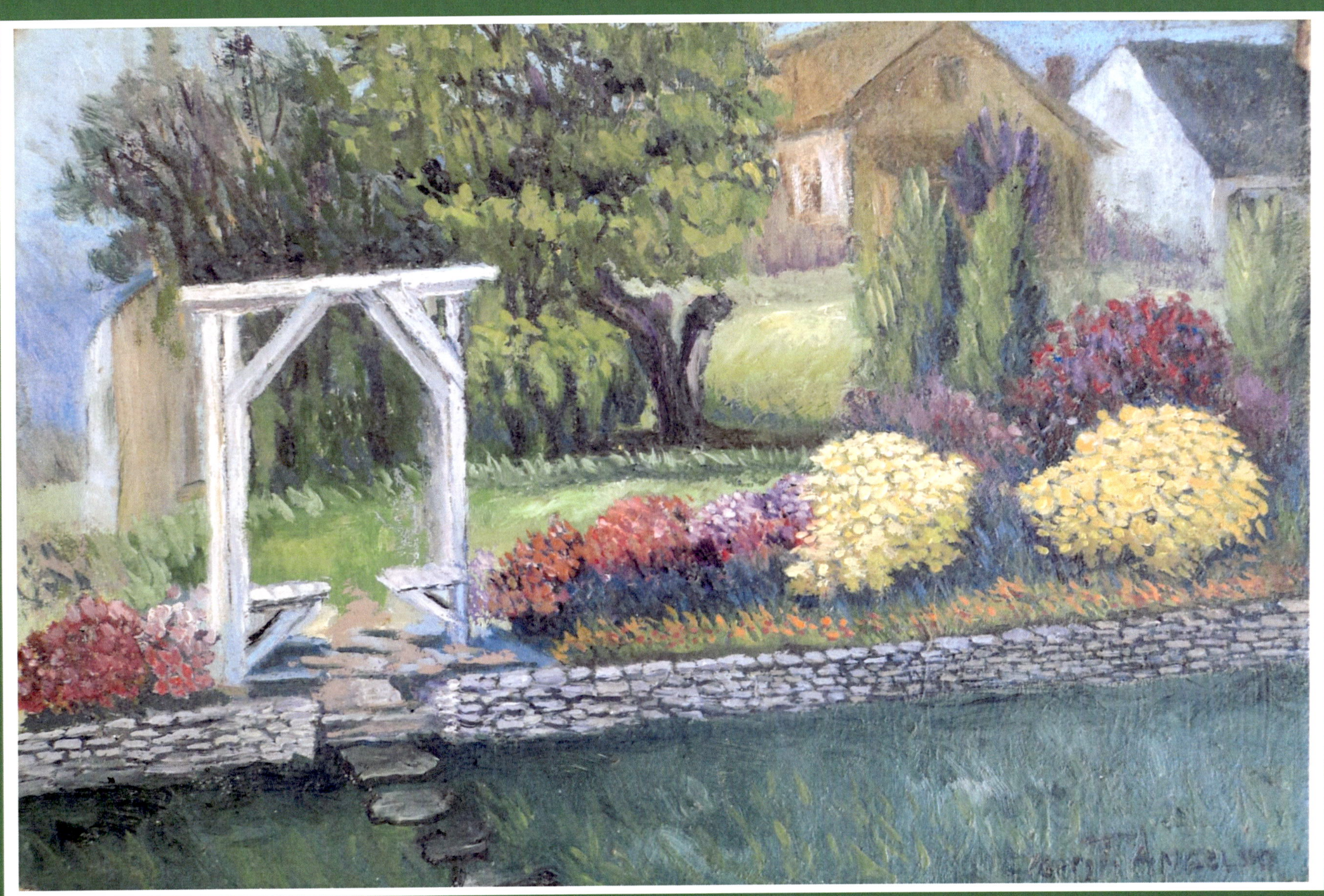

The season's flowers reach their peak of brilliant color.

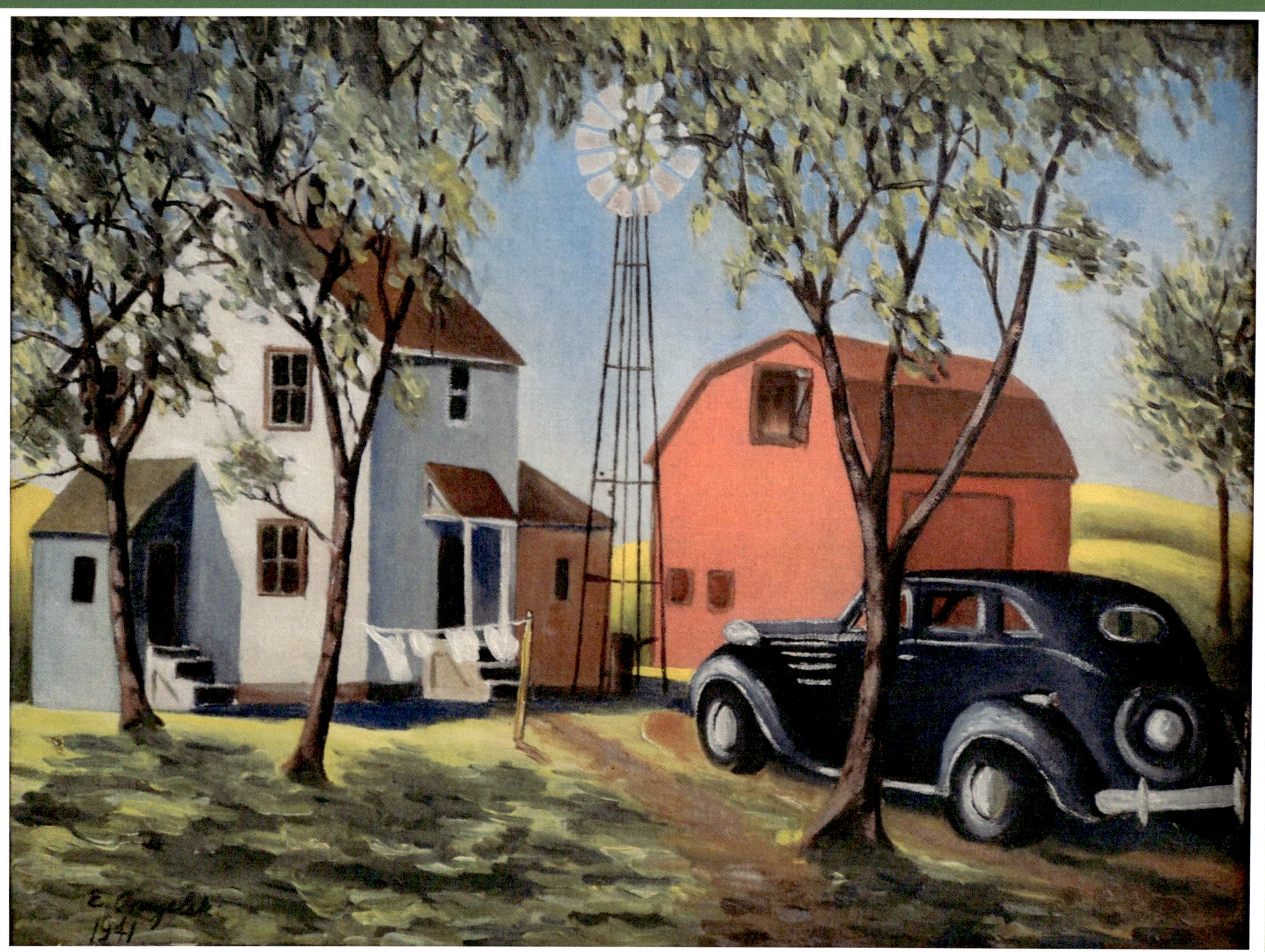

E. Gorgoss
1941

❖ *Let me remember you, voices of little insects,*

*Weeds in the moonlight, fields that are tangled with asters,*

*Let me remember, soon will the winter be on us,*

> *Snow-hushed and heavy.*

*Over my soul murmur your mute benediction,*

*While I gaze, O fields that rest after harvest,*

*As those who part look long in the eyes they lean to,*

> *Lest they forget them.*

—Sara Teasdale
"September Midnight" (excerpt)

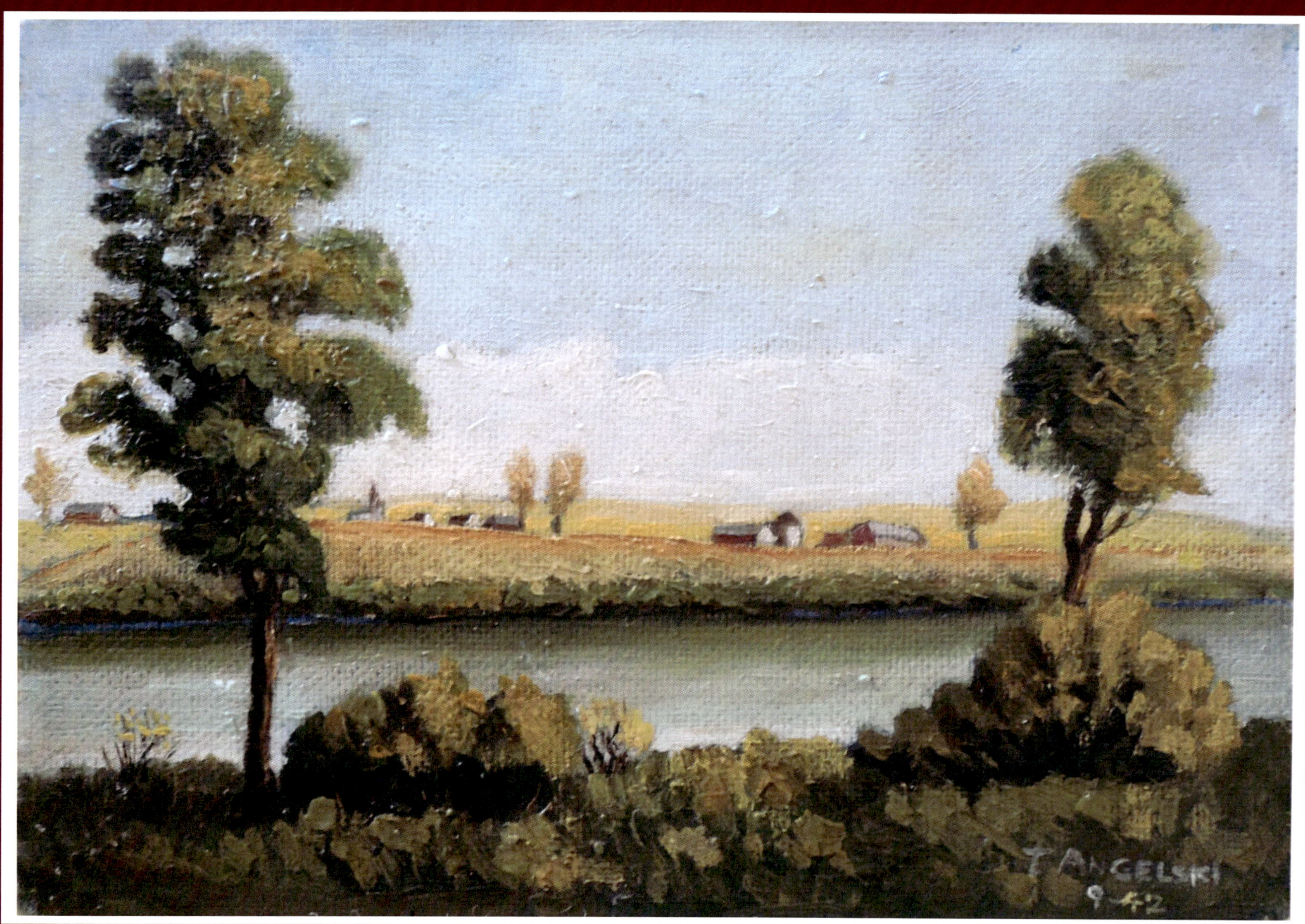
J. Angelski
9-42

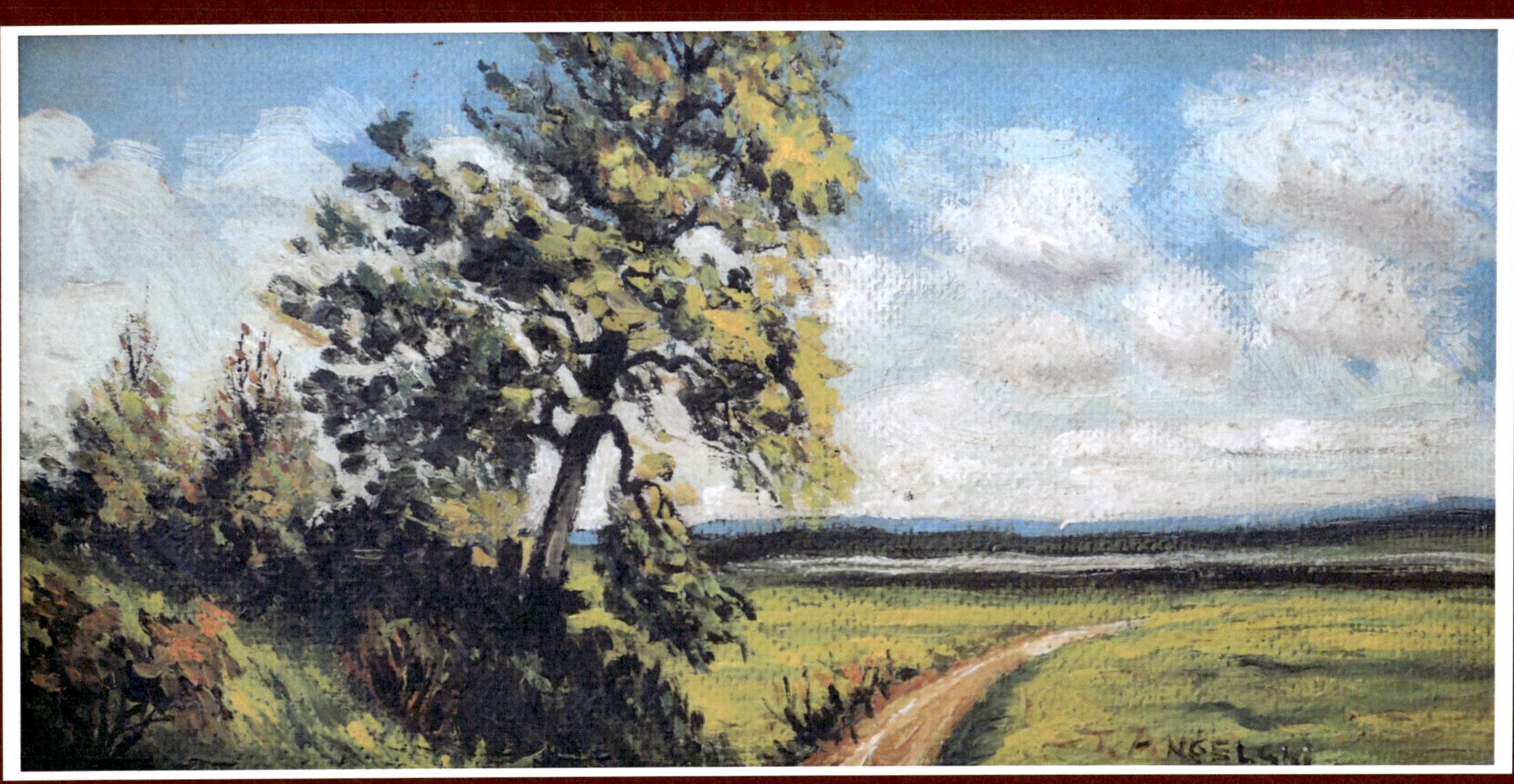

J. Engelen

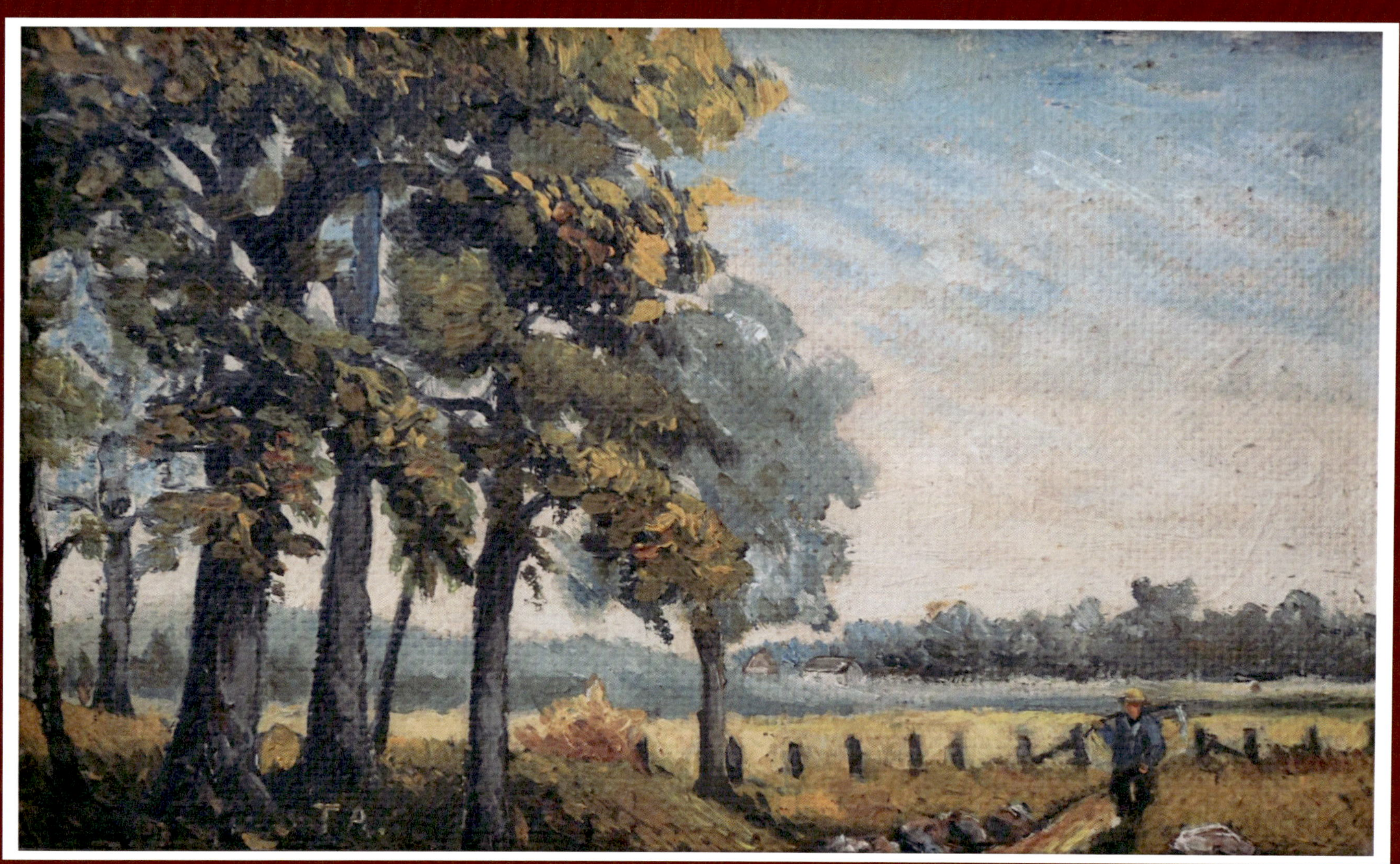



Harvesting the crops makes for a long but satisfying day's work in the field.

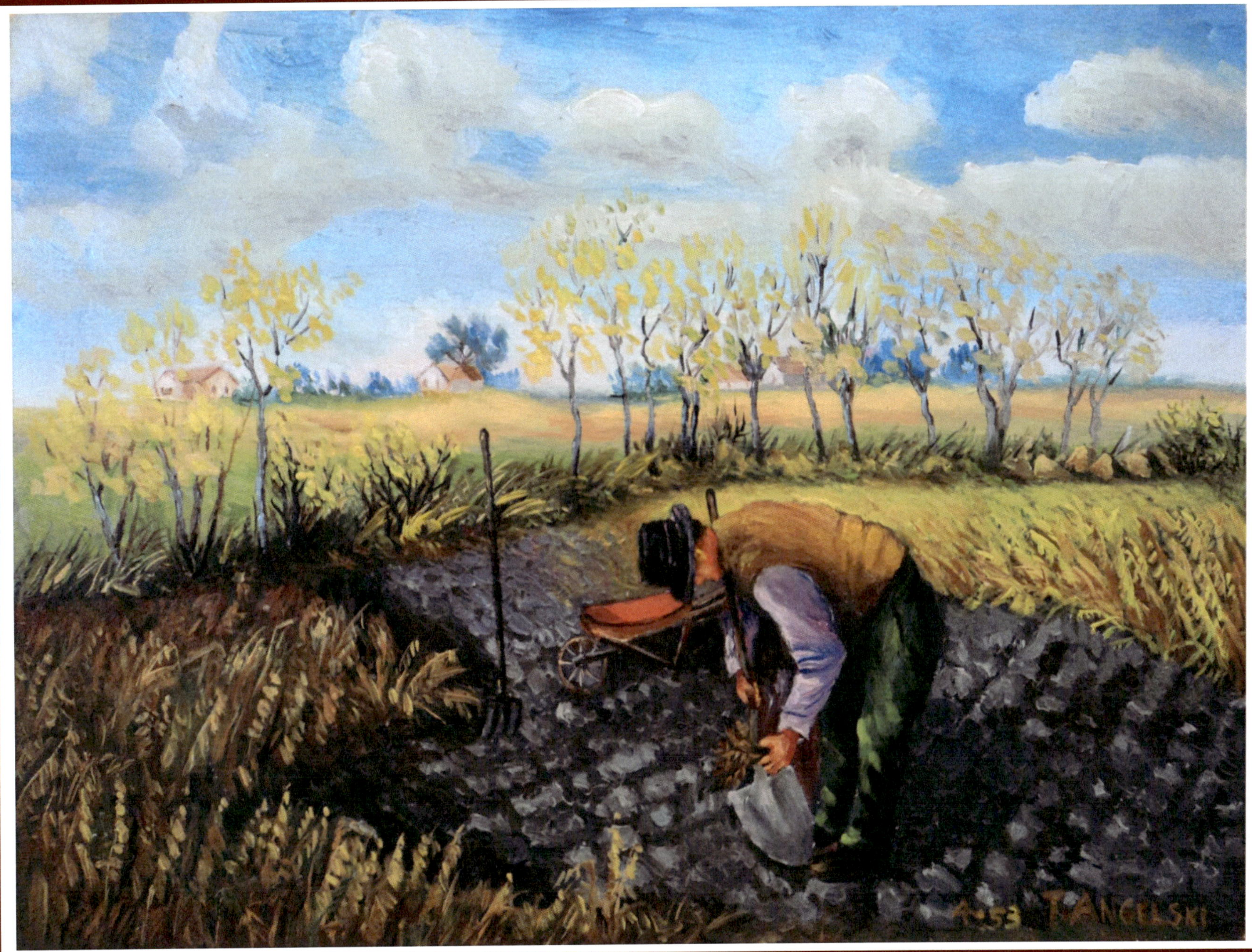

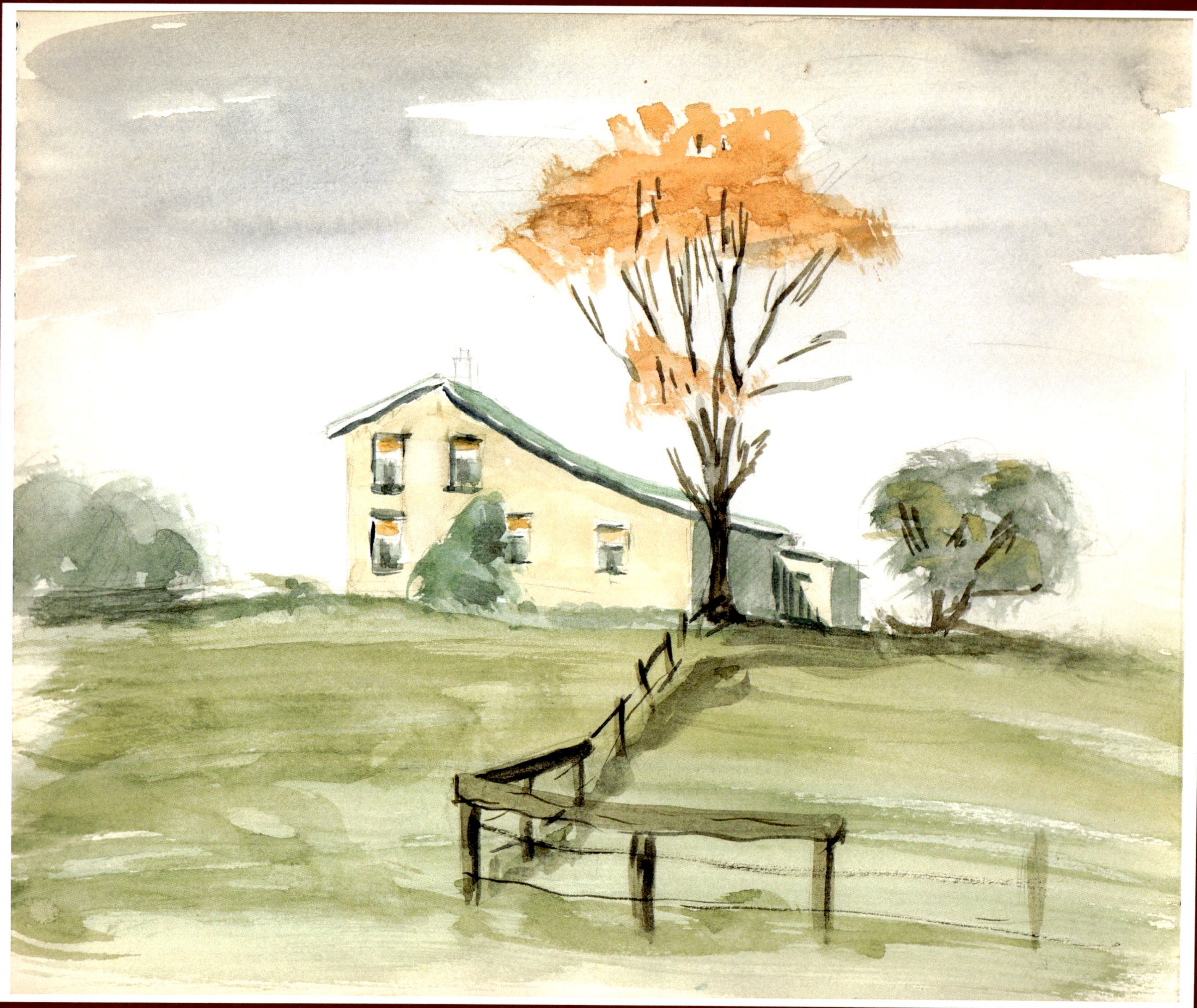

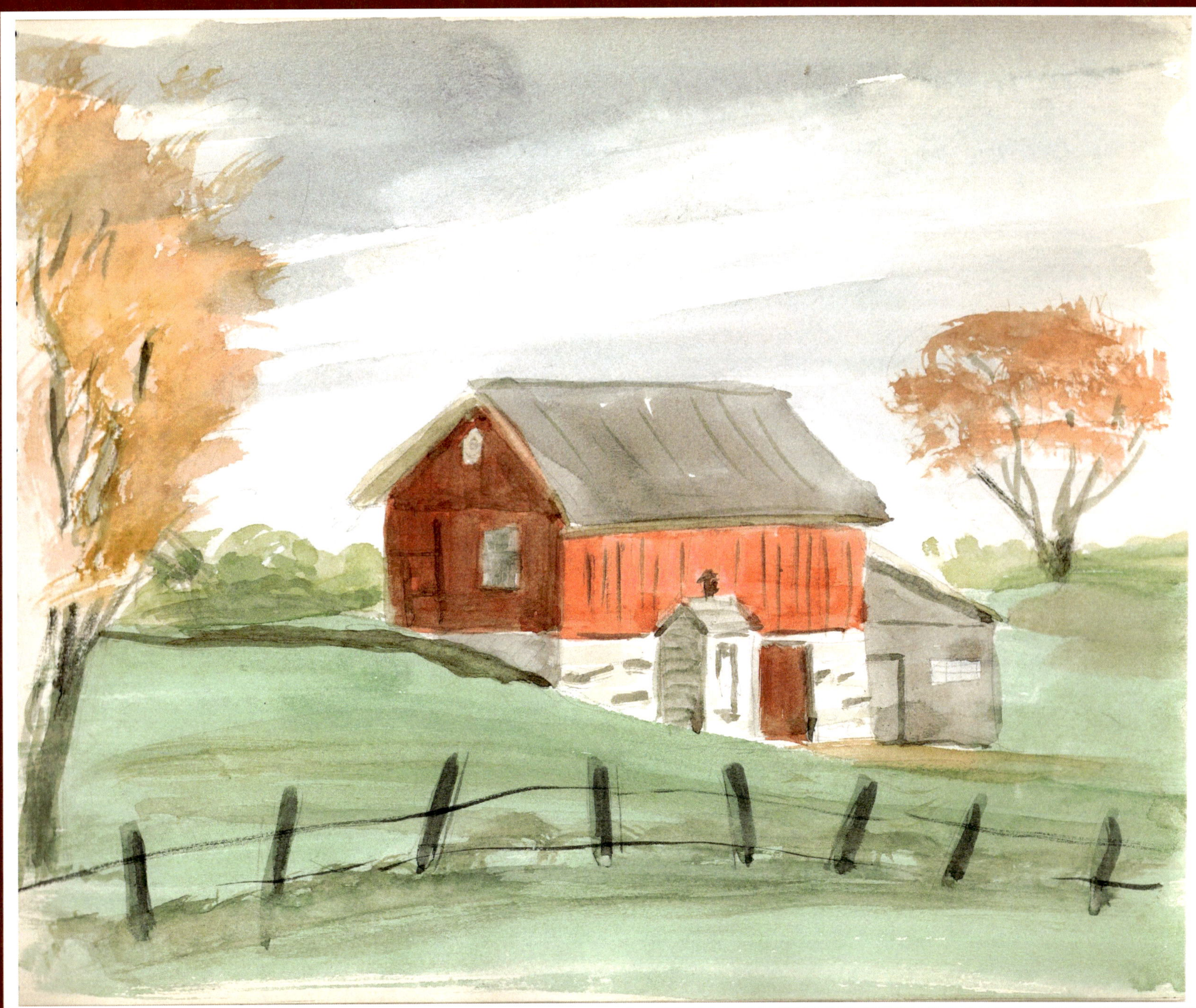

Orange hues reveal that autumn is in full swing.

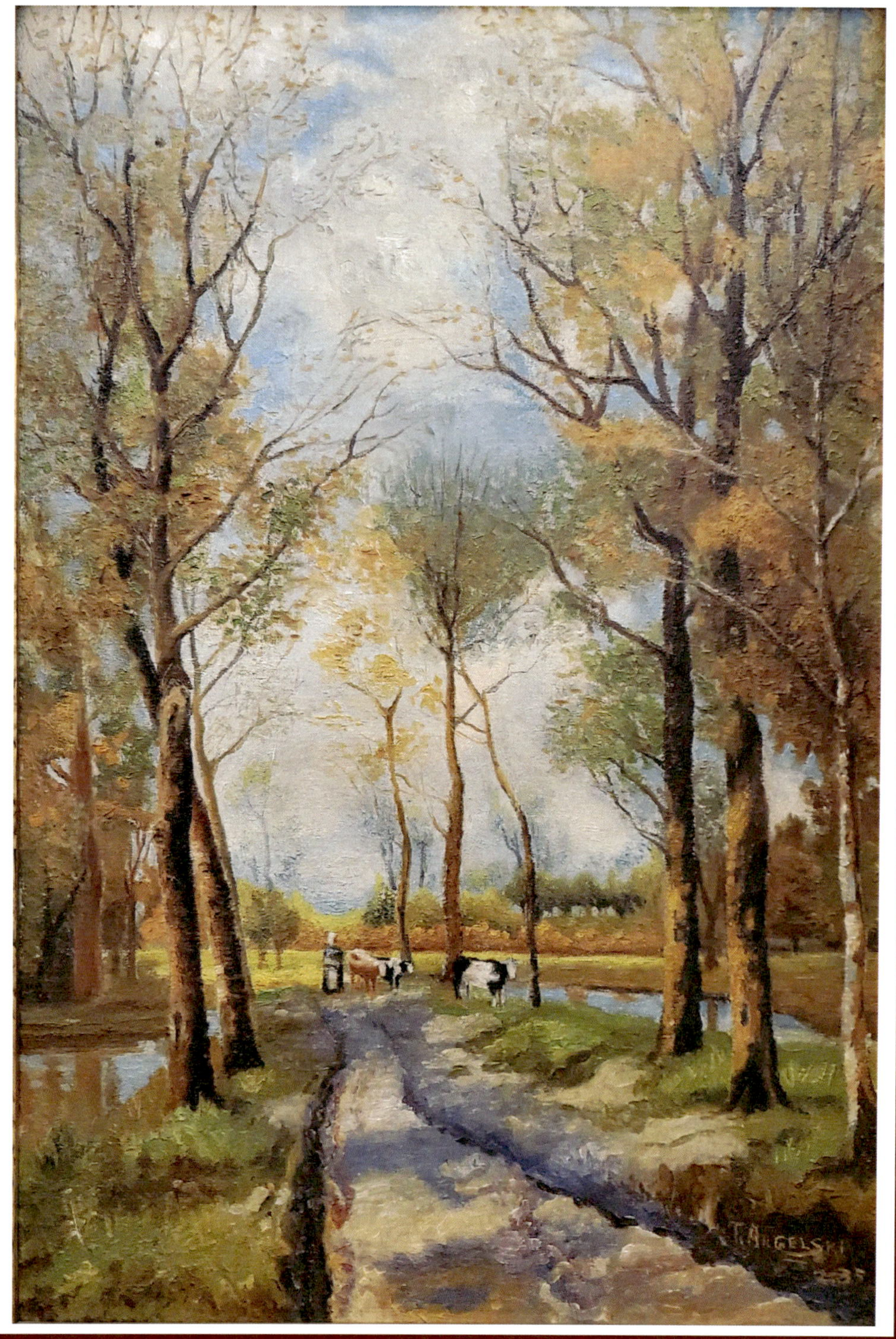

Leaves become sparser on the trees as farm animals feel the seasonal change in the air.

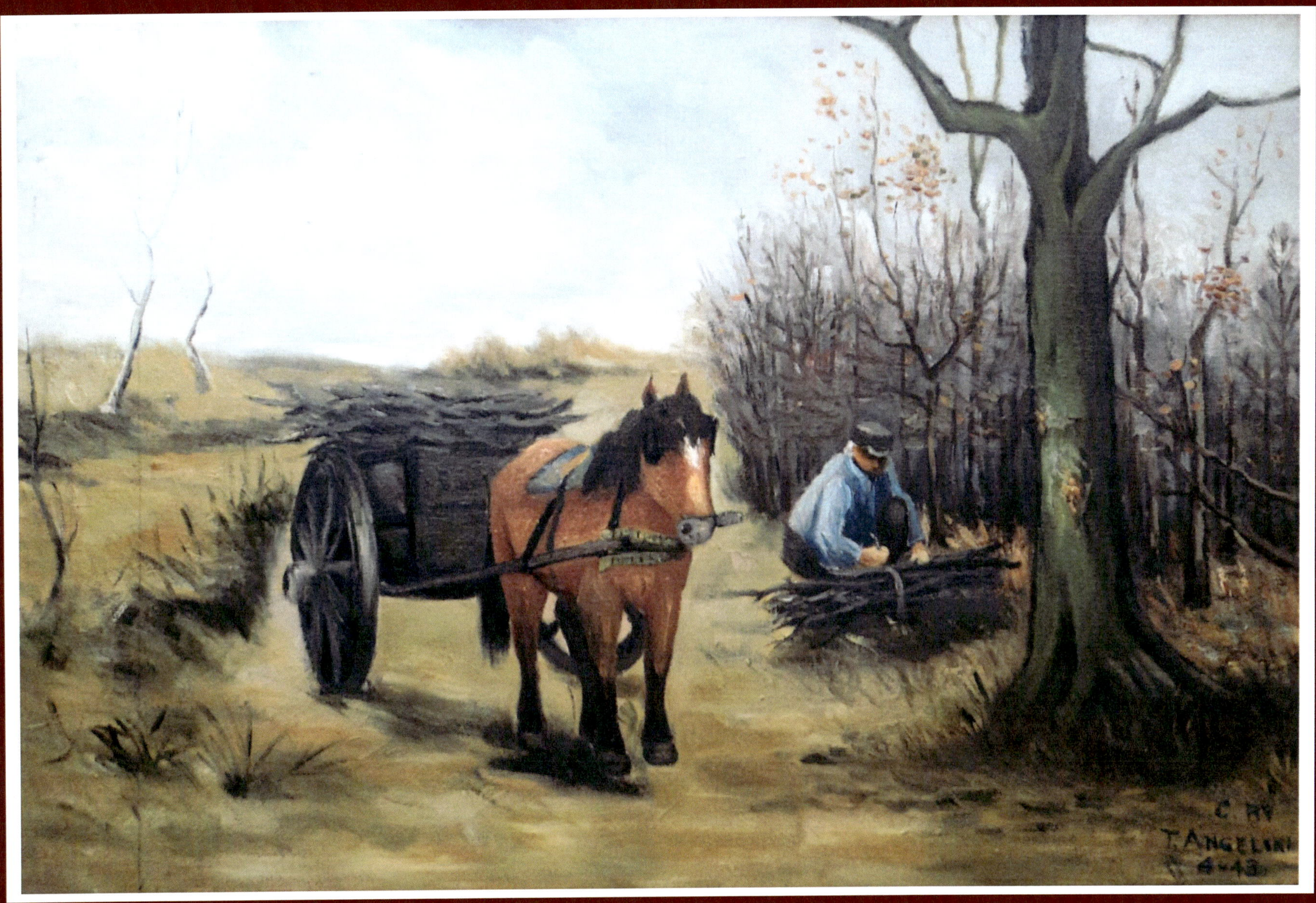




Wood must be gathered, cut, bundled, and carted away for storage or burned in the fireplace that evening.

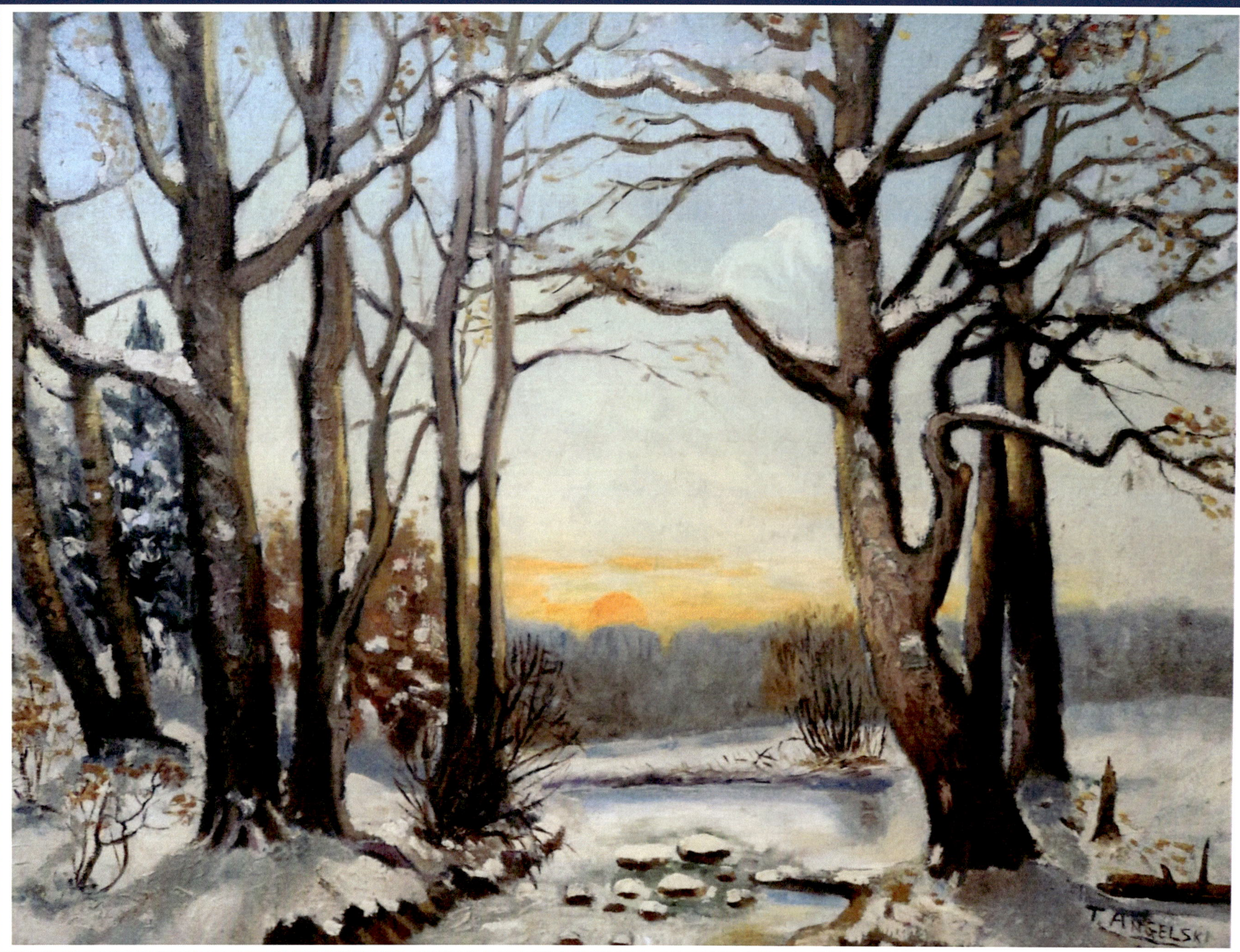

T. ANGELSKI

Sunset or sunrise? However you see it, the sun's distant golden glow makes us think of some of the year's shortest days. Its rays have done little to melt the snow nestled on these branches and the sheet of ice that coats the creek. Clear skies suggest that the air is crisp but calm, as one can hear the jeer of a blue jay from a faraway pine. It is the only sound that can be heard for miles since the soft crunch of snow underfoot subsided when we stopped to admire the scene. The day and year draw to a close, or they begin anew.

# ABOUT THE ARTISTS

Thomas Angelski was born in the heart of Chicago's North Side Polish neighborhood in 1884 to immigrant parents Andrew Angielski and Regina nee Zaucha. An appreciation for art and craftsmanship was instilled in him at an early age from his father, a bicycle maker, and his mother, who had artistic and musical talent. Tragically, his mother died after childbirth when Thomas was nine years old. As an escape from Chicago's smokestacks and stockyards as well as his changing home environment, Thomas at times walked from his home to see exhibits at the Chicago Art Institute. However, it was many years before he applied his own artistic ability.

After Thomas's father remarried, his family moved near Benton Harbor, Michigan, for about a year. Then they arrived in Wisconsin, settling on a farm near the Town of Abrams almost twenty miles

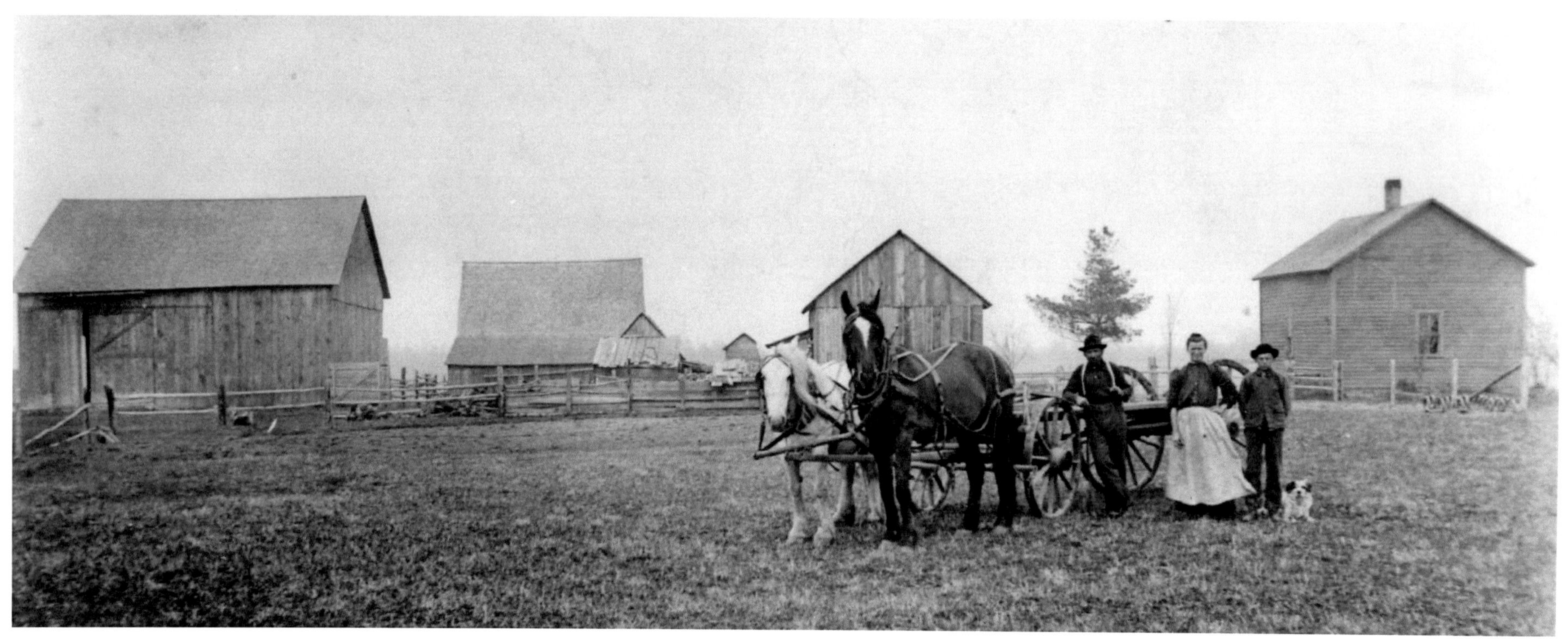

The farm of Andrew Angielski near Abrams

north of Green Bay. Thomas found work at a local sawmill, later became the foreman of a railroad crew, and eventually purchased his own farm. He married Antoinette (Anna) Pietrowiak in 1909 and they moved to Milwaukee, where Thomas became a skilled machinist.

Thomas and Anna had seven children, all born between 1910 and 1920. Although he was a busy family man, Thomas regularly made time to take his boys to see the permanent collection at the Layton Art Gallery. This instilled an appreciation for art in his children, most of whom displayed talent in some form of artwork themselves.

As his children grew older, Thomas set up his easel in the kitchen of their South Side home to practice oil painting. Landscapes were his favorite artistic subject, and his realistic style is evident in the single brush strokes of detail and texture he added to them. Occasionally, Thomas also made pieces of furniture and carved small figures.

In 1940, when Thomas's son Eugene went to the Layton School of Art to register for classes, the director Charlotte Partridge spoke with Thomas about his own interest in art. After urging him to bring in some of his paintings, she was so impressed that she created a scholarship for him to attend art classes at night.

Although he was in his forties when he began to develop his skill of oil painting, Thomas continued to paint until he was nearly eighty years old. Over fifty of his paintings have been located, spanning various themes and styles, but many others are known to exist. A selection of Thomas's paintings was displayed at an art exhibit at the Polish Center of Wisconsin in Franklin in the fall of 2013.

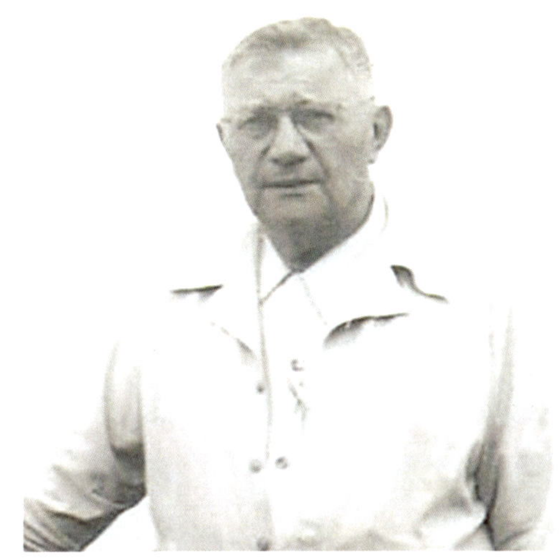

Thomas Angelski

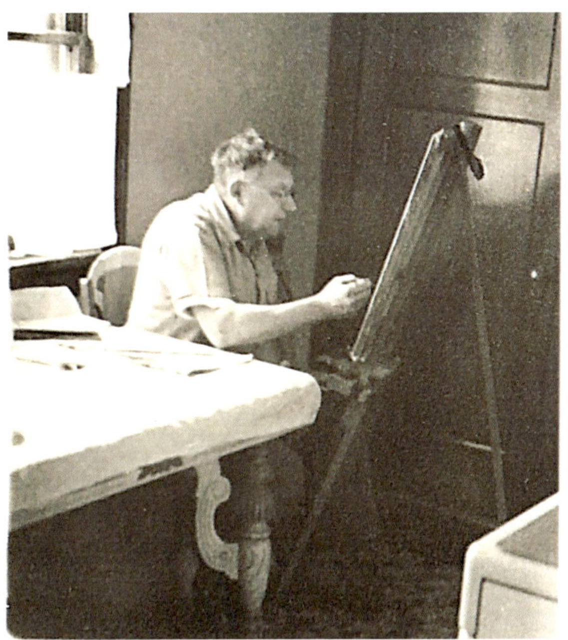

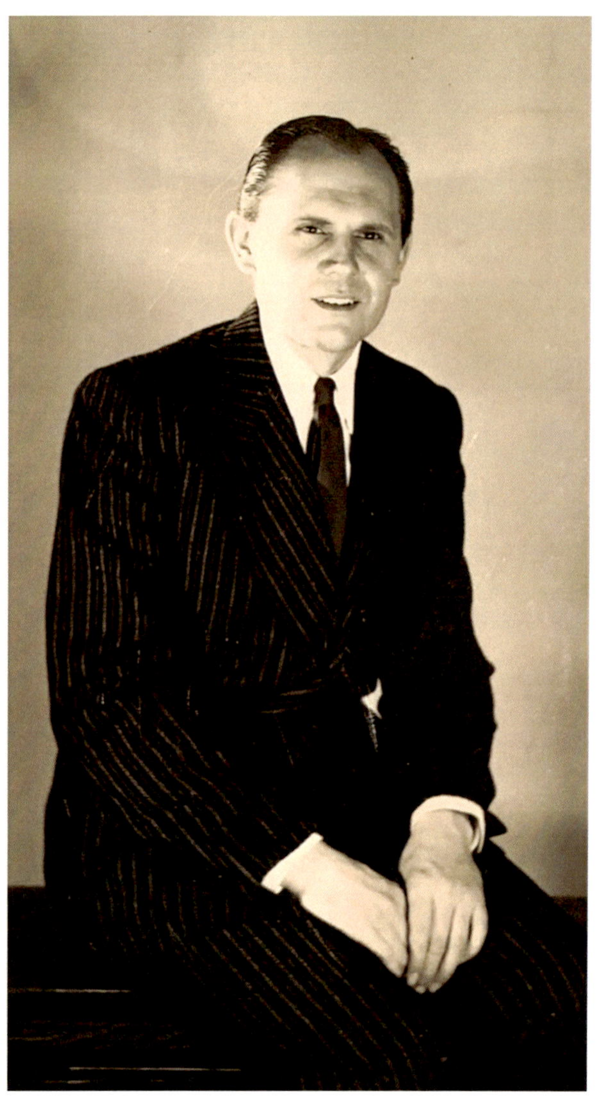

Edward Angell

Thomas and Anna's oldest son Edward was born in 1910 in Milwaukee. At age fifteen, Edward began working as a barber—a career that lasted over eighty years. For most of those years, he worked at his North Side barbershop near his home. Edward styled both hair and hairpieces for a variety of clients, including distinguished ones. Even at the age of ninety-six, he still cut hair part-time.

In the early 1940's, Edward took art lessons at a studio in Downtown Milwaukee. He filled sketchbooks with watercolor scenes from his travels throughout Wisconsin and enjoyed the art of photography as well. Several of Edward's watercolors were inspired by the landscape near his wife Angeline's hometown of Coleman, north of Green Bay. In later years, Edward learned to design stained glass. He and his family members took great pride in his ornate glass handiwork that decorated their home.

Edward and Angeline raised a daughter and a son. Edward's passion for art later passed down to his grandson Brett Angell, who works at the Museum of Fine Arts, Boston, and has received critical acclaim for his own diverse body of artwork.

Eugene was the second youngest of Thomas and Anna's children, born in Milwaukee in 1919. He demonstrated a love for art at an early age and enrolled at the Layton School of Art after graduating from high school. When faced with the World War II draft, however, Eugene chose to enlist for the U.S. Air Force.

Eugene was deployed to North Africa, where he worked on aircraft repairs and modifications. His reputation as an artist earned him the role of painting nose art on some of the bombers. Eugene's military excursions also took him to Italy, where he observed Rome's greatest Renaissance masterpieces in person. Everywhere he went, he brought his sketchbook and a tiny case for watercolors, creating vivid scenes of both military and civilian life.

After coming home to Milwaukee, Eugene returned to the Layton School of Art, where he practiced the techniques he learned from the artist and instructor Edmund Lewandowski. Eugene then applied for a veteran's scholarship to study art at Scripps College in Claremont, California. Once accepted there, he studied under the renowned painter Millard Sheets. The art theory Eugene learned at Scripps College shaped the unique style he expressed on wood, paper, and canvas for the rest of his life.

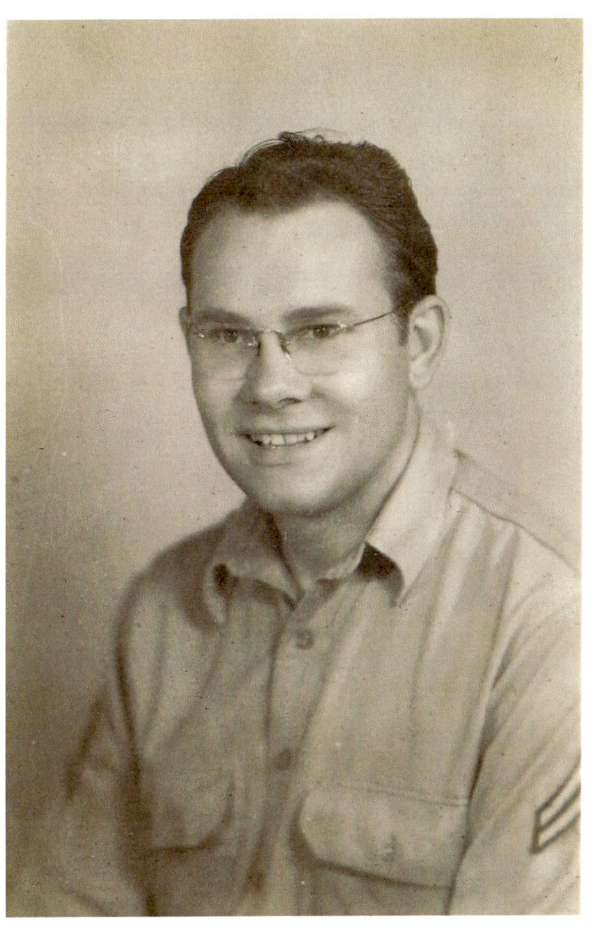

Eugene Angelski

Eugene married Barbara Hoover in 1950, and they raised two sons. After he retired from the Lockheed Corporation, he and his wife moved to the hills near Prescott, Arizona, where the desert scenery and culture provided an abundance of artistic inspiration. Perhaps Eugene's greatest work was his seven-foot-tall painted wood carving *The Cowboy and the Calf* that drew acclaim through his local newspaper. As the longest-surviving Angelski sibling, Eugene died in 2017 at the age of ninety-eight.

<u>E N D N O T E S</u>

All locations mentioned are in Wisconsin.

1. Edward Angell, watercolor, 1942-1943. Near Highway 100 and West Hampton Avenue, Milwaukee.

2. Edward Angell, watercolor, 1940's.

3. Thomas Angelski, oil, 1956. View from the rear of the artist's property just north of General Mitchell Field (the current Mitchell International Airport), Milwaukee.

4. Thomas Angelski, oil, 1944. The Milwaukee River in Downtown Milwaukee looking north toward the Michigan Street Bridge. The painting features several historic landmarks, including Gimbels Department Store (white building on the left), the Pabst Building in the center (later replaced by the Faison Building), and the First Wisconsin National Bank behind it.

5. Edward Angell, watercolor, 1943. The Highland Bar (center), an old-fashioned corner tavern that was located just east of where the Fiserv Forum now stands in Downtown Milwaukee. This was about a block away from the studio where Edward took art classes.

6. Edward Angell, watercolor, 1943. The Cathedral of St. John the Evangelist, Milwaukee. The darkened color of this iconic landmark—viewed from across Cathedral Square—was accurately portrayed here six decades before the Cream City brick exterior was cleaned and restored to its original appearance.

7, 8. Edward Angell, watercolor, 1943. Farm scenes along Highway YY (Pilgrim Road), near Brookfield and Menomonee Falls.

9. Eugene Angelski, acrylic, 1940's. View from the artist's upstairs window on South 24th Street, depicting the densely populated Clarke Square neighborhood on Milwaukee's South Side.

10. Edward Angell, watercolor, 1940's. View across from the artist's barbershop on West Lloyd Street in the Washington Heights neighborhood of Milwaukee's North Side.

11. Edward Angell, watercolor, 1940's.

12, 13, 14. Edward Angell, watercolor, 1940's.

15. Edward Angell, watercolor, 1943.

16. Edward Angell, sketch and watercolor, 1943. Farm buildings in the Town of Lake—a large area of southeastern Milwaukee County later developed into suburban neighborhoods of well-maintained properties.

17, 18. Edward Angell, watercolor, 1942. Farm scenes near Coleman, Marinette County.

19, 20. Edward Angell, watercolor, 1940's. Near Walnut and Commerce Streets, Milwaukee. The modern-day location is near the Pleasant Street Bridge over the Milwaukee River in the Brewer's Hill neighborhood north of downtown.

21. Thomas Angelski, oil, 1940. The clubhouse at McKinley Marina, Milwaukee, three years before it was destroyed by fire.

22, 23. Edward Angell, watercolor, 1942. Pewaukee Lake and Lac La Belle, near Oconomowoc.

24. Edward Angell, watercolor, 1943.

25. Eugene Angelski, sketch, 1947. Port Washington maritime scene of a fishing tugboat passing the row of shanties along the west slip.

26, 27. Edward Angell, watercolor, 1940's.

28. Eugene Angelski, watercolor, 1947. Near Thiensville, Ozaukee County.

29. Edward Angell, watercolor, 1943. Country lane near Coleman.

30, 31. Eugene Angelski, watercolor, 1940's. Near Hales Corners.

32. Eugene Angelski, watercolor, 1940's. Farmland in Greenfield. The house in this picture stood next to six acres owned by the Angelski family off West Layton Avenue. The fields they quietly cultivated are now partly occupied by the heavily traveled I-43 Airport Freeway.

33. Eugene Angelski, watercolor, 1940's. The Mitchell Park Conservatory. Many years later, the structure pictured was replaced by the well-known three glass domes on the same site.

34, 35. Edward Angell, watercolor, 1942. Farm buildings near Abrams, Oconto County. When Edward returned to the area he knew from his youth, he found the old farmhouse boarded up and long abandoned.

36, 37. Thomas Angelski, oil, 1937. Farm scenes in Franklin. These two paintings show features of the property on South 51st Street where a niece of Thomas lived: the farmhouse, milk house (painted red), summer kitchen, and marshy fields.

38. Edward Angell, watercolor, 1940's.

39. Edward Angell, watercolor, 1940's. Cobblestone Hotel, East Troy. This painting, though unfinished, captures a landmark—also called the Buena Vista House—that stood 175 years until its demolition in 2022.

40. Thomas Angelski, oil, 1959. The backyard of the artist's home on South Taylor Avenue, Milwaukee. The wooden trellis pictured here was one of Thomas's own creations.

41. Eugene Angelski, acrylic, 1941. Rural scene. This painting illustrates Eugene's contemporary style in contrast with his father's tendency toward realism. It also demonstrates two of Eugene's favorite artistic concepts: First, he chose contrasting *colors*, perfectly placed, to generate interest in his subject. Would it not be a less compelling scene if the sunlit fields behind the red barn lacked their yellow luster? Second, note how his use of *shapes* prompts us to explore the painting from one object to the next: The angles in the farmhouse roof act like arrows that point toward the center. The windmill directs our gaze toward the foliage, and the branches invite our eyes back down toward the barn and automobile. These methods serve to capture our attention and hold it until we have observed each element of the scene.

42. Thomas Angelski, oil, 1942. Near Jefferson. While some artists may prefer to use trees only as a backdrop for the main subject, Thomas composed this scene with the tree line in front. This forms a natural frame for the river and the farms dotting the autumn landscape in the distance.

43, 44. Thomas Angelski, oil, year unknown. Wooded scenes. In these two paintings, trees occupy the foreground, while a curving path transports us to the golden fields in the background. In the first painting, there was something about this tree that convinced Thomas it could stand as the subject of the scene itself: the crooked angle at which it grew from the side of the hill. In the second painting, a man returns from his day's work in the field. Observe carefully and you will find his blue coat appearing again on one of the following pages.

45. Thomas Angelski, oil, 1953. Harvest scene reminiscent of the fields near Abrams from Thomas's past. Could the farmer in this painting be his younger self?

46. Edward Angell, watercolor, 1942. Farmhouse near Coleman.

47. Edward Angell, watercolor, 1942. Farm near Coleman. Complete with rolling hills, red barn, and wooden post fence, this is the quintessential Wisconsin scene from the 1940's.

48. Thomas Angelski, oil, 1935.

49. Thomas Angelski, oil, 1943. As displayed throughout this book, Thomas's art featured trees prominently. He was not merely depicting something he had observed in nature; he painted what he knew best from handling lumber at the sawmill day after day. Eugene, who remembered this painting on his father's easel, expounded at the age of ninety-four:

"Dad knew trees. He would line up the tree, cut off all the loose branches, and take a saw. Then on the ground, he'd trim the tree off and make a good clean cut, and he got a lot of lumber out of that tree. He was a real guy of many trades. He was original. He painted the way he saw it, right there out there in the wilderness."

50. Thomas Angelski, oil, 1936.

<u>W O R K S   C O N S U L T E D</u>


Angelski, Eugene. Personal interview conducted by Michael and Collene Angelski. 16 Sept. 2013.

Angelski family documents from the collections of Clare Ann Gaouette and Michael Grudzielanek.

"Demo of East Troy's Historic Cobblestone Inn Underway." <u>Lake Geneva News</u> 12 May 2022.

Dunbar, Paul Laurence. "In Summer Time." *The Complete Poems of Paul Laurence Dunbar*, Dodd, Mead and Company, 1913, pp. 280-281.

"Father Wins Art School Scholarship." <u>Milwaukee Journal</u> 22 May 1940: Green Sheet, p. 1.

Hope, Andrew. <u>Architecture of Faith: Chapter I - Catholic Cathedral of St. John the Evangelist</u>. 2017. 23 Jan. 2024. <http://www.architectureoffaithmilwaukee.info>.

Stevens, Wallace. "The Snow Man." *The Collected Poems of Wallace Stevens*, Alfred A. Knopf, 1954, p. 9.

Stingl, Jim. "Shear Persistence." <u>Milwaukee Journal</u> 31 Mar. 2006: B1+.

Teasdale, Sara. "September Midnight." *Poetry: A Magazine of Verse, Vol. III, No. VI*, Harriet Monroe, Mar. 1914, p. 201.

"Watercolor Class Makes State Jaunts." <u>Milwaukee Sentinel</u> 13 July 1947: 6C.

Williams, William Carlos. "Spring and All." *The Collected Poems of William Carlos Williams: Volume I, 1909-1939*, edited by A. Walton Litz and Christopher MacGowan, New Directions, 1986, p. 183.

www.ingramcontent.com/pod-product-compliance
Lightning Source LLC
Chambersburg PA
CBRC101058120726
48010CB00014B/366